HEALTHY COCKTAILS

HEALTHY COCKTAILS

Easy & Fun Recipes for All-Natural,
Low-Sugar, Low-Alcohol Drinks

MATT DORSEY &
JENNY DORSEY

Skyhorse Publishing

Skyhorse Publishing books may be purchased in bulk at special discounts for sales promotion, corporate gifts, fund-raising, or educational purposes. Special editions can also be created to specifications. For details, contact the Special Sales Department, Skyhorse Publishing, 307 West 36th Street, 11th Floor, New York, NY 10018 or info@skyhorsepublishing.com.

Skyhorse® and Skyhorse Publishing® are registered trademarks of Skyhorse Publishing, Inc.®, a Delaware corporation.

Visit our website at www.skyhorsepublishing.com.

10 9 8 7 6 5 4 3 2 1

Library of Congress Cataloging-in-Publication Data is available on file.

Cover design by Laura Klynstra and Brian Peterson
Cover photo credit: Jenny Dorsey

Print ISBN: 978-1-5107-4494-3
Ebook ISBN: 978-1-5107-4495-0

Printed in China

To those like me who shied away from their creativity: let it loose!
—Matt

CONTENTS

INTRODUCTION

At its core, cocktail culture is about relaxing, sipping on something delicious, and having a bit of fun. That spirit guides our interpretation of healthy in this book, too: combining the goodness of less-processed, lower-calorie, and more nutritionally dense ingredients with both classic and experimental styles of beverage to take the edge off without compromising any New Year's resolutions or fitness goals. To me, having control over every part of the cocktail—from choosing quality liquor to mastering flavorful infusions, tinctures, and syrups—is the best way to maximize taste without sacrificing flavor and enjoyment.

I don't wish a life of vodka-sodas on anyone, but I do appreciate the simplicity of that drink. That's why the recipes in this book are unfussy and easy to whip up for either a solo tipple or a group gathering. They also emphasize freshness in the form of juices or whole fruits and vegetables. I've also taken refined sugar out of the equation by making syrups from natural alternatives like monk fruit or xylitol (derived from birch trees), removing premade mixers, and shying away from high-sugar liqueurs and amaros. In some instances, I've removed the alcohol altogether in favor of zero-proof mocktails that are still multilayered and flavorful but contain few to no calories. This does require a little bit of extra effort, but I think it's well worth it in delicious liquid results.

Living a healthy life necessitates a sustainable lifestyle, and these cocktails aim to find that balance of allowing some indulgences without causing you to guiltily reflect back on a night's fun. I hope you enjoy the heck out of each beverage, knowing you don't need to count calories, and learn some novel new techniques and tricks along the way. Ultimately, these recipes are meant to set a foundation for healthy cocktails, and I leave it up to you to imbue them with your own whims and personality, whether you choose a more seasonally appropriate fruit for a smash or switch up a spice for a syrup. The possibilities are endless, which is why I've concocted this useful flavor profile and cocktail-style matrix to help categorize the recipes of this book and serve as a jumping-off point for your own future creations.

HOW TO USE THIS BOOK

Flavor Profiles

Fruit	Herbal	Wood	Chemical
Citrus	Floral	Spicy	Earthy
Tropical	Medicinal	Sweet	Mineral
Stone	Fresh	Nutty	Fermented
Berry	Vegetal	Smoky	Boozy

Cocktail Styles

Fruit	Herbal	Wood	Chemical
Smash	Julep	Manhattan	Negroni
Daquiri	Martini	Old-Fashioned	Sazerac
Colada	Gimlet	Dark N Stormy	Boulevardier
Margarita	Bloody Mary	Penicillin	Toddy
Caipirinha	Mojito		
Paloma			

Cocktails in this Book

	Fruit	Herbal	Wood	Chemical
Vodka	A-"Pear"-itif	Bone Broth Bloody "Bull" Cilantro Celery Collins Beets & Basil Saved by the Bell Fennel Turmeric Shooter	Moscow Mule Pumpkin Matcha Fizz	
Gin	Spicy Bee's Knees Raspberry Sour Tom Collins Ramos Gin Fizz	Eat Your Peas! Gotham Sunset Isle of Capri		Beer's Knees
Rum	Coconut Water Colada Daiquiri Frozen Strawberry "Daiquiri" Mango Adventures"	Avo "Toast"	Dark 'N' Stormy Spiced Rum Milk Punch Cuba Libre	
Bourbon	Blackberry Smash Brown Derby Southern Blessing	Green & Black Mint Julep	Five-Spice Old-Fashioned Ginger Melon Shooter	
Other Whiskey	Tart Cherry Switchel Shooter	Activated	Golden Penicillin Pistachio-Date Punch	Hot Toddy Ode to Orkney
Tequila/Mezcal	Watermelon Mint Cooler Sugar-Free Paloma Recoverita	Hibiscus Lessons from Nica	Milk-Free Spiced Latte	
Other Spirits		The Green Hour	Applejack Tea	Oceana
Nonalcoholic	Taste of the Tropics New Age Pimm's Cup	Mulled "Wine"		

Photo credit: Dion Trinidad

MARATHONS & MIXOLOGY
About the Mixologist

The first time I ever served a cocktail to anyone besides myself and my then-girlfriend, now-wife, Jenny, was at our inaugural pop-up dinner. That was back in 2014, many moons and hundreds of events ago, when the two of us first had the (slightly harebrained) idea to start hosting food- and drink-centric events. We started first out of our home, gathering small groups of people who wanted something deeper and more thoughtful than the regular ol' weather-and-subway conversation, then slowly migrated into venues across the world (some of my personal favorites include an island hotel in Nicaragua, an abandoned warehouse in San Francisco, and a multi-floor museum in NYC). You could say it was the ultimate trial by fire; not only was this an exercise in vulnerability and openness for me—I was doing something I was actively interested in but completely new to sharing with others—but it was also a learning curve to see if and how Jenny and I could work together to build something to bring out both our creative sides.

I still remember what I made: two cocktails, one called Cloak & Swagger, the other Oriental, both from the secret recipe book of mixologist Greg Best (then of Atlanta's Holeman and Finch Public House). Until I had met him a year or so prior, I only considered myself a good drinker—not particularly discerning, nor particularly interested in knowing more. When I wandered into his bar, right around the corner from where I lived, his obvious love for craft cocktails and deep knowledge of the space pulled me in immediately. When you ordered any drink, he would tell you its origin story, how he made every single ingredient—bitters, syrups, infusions—and why it made sense for the ethos of his bar. That was a clear delineation for me, learning the rich and complex history behind the alcohols I enjoyed and realizing the enjoyment of drinking isn't at all about maximizing the volume of alcohol being consumed. I found myself at Greg's bar at least a few times a week just listening, watching, absorbing. As I was leaving the city to move up north, he gifted me with a recipe book containing dozens of his and other mixologists' tried-and-true recipes as a way to help me muster up the courage to make and serve drinks to others.

Even with his book, my first cocktail service did not go so well. I followed every recipe to a T, yet they just didn't taste the way I remembered. Everything was too boozy, and the balance was just wrong somehow. I felt open and exposed, bringing a tray of these cocktails-in-progress to new people who could certainly judge me. But I'd be damned if I let that fear, that pressure, dampen something I could feel had grabbed me. So I got to work, researching everything I could about cocktails: first liquors; then liqueurs, amaros, and other odd ingredients; styles of drinks; the golden ratio and when to break it. I made every single one of the recipes in the book until I struck a rhythm between pours, stirs, and shakes as the balance of each cocktail slowly became muscle memory and not a strain. I was able to wean off riffing on others' recipes to creating my own for the last four or so years now (there's a story about that later in the book too), and after making tens of thousands of drinks, I can say definitively there have been some great ones and some terrible ones, but all of them have been part of the most fun ride I could've ever dreamed up for a formerly self-described "noncreative type."

Alongside my journey as a mixologist has also been my growth as a marathon runner. While being active and healthy has always been part of my DNA—growing up, I was always outside playing basketball, then I went through an era of mixed martial arts and weight lifting—things really fell into place when I started running. I was fresh out of college and looking for an exercise outlet when a colleague of mine mentioned she was running a half marathon. Being the (slight) extremist that I am, I figured *why not go for the full one*? That was ten years ago. My first full marathon was Nashville, the next Savannah, then New Orleans. It didn't take long to fully integrate races into my life, which naturally led me to set a goal for myself to complete the 51 in 50 (50 marathons in 50 states, plus Washington, DC).

I'm now nineteen marathons in, and I'll be honest: juggling these two particular passions of mine has not come easily. When Jenny and I were "doing research" by going to cocktail bars, I often felt frustrated because I couldn't imbibe more freely due to my marathon schedule and diet. The high amount of sugars in certain cocktail ingredients—especially amaros and liqueurs—became a pain point for me as I contemplated having another at the bar. As a result, I began working on a subset of feel-good, better-for-you cocktails I could shake up when I was training for my next race that wouldn't physically—and mentally—come bite me later. With that, my cocktail style had organically evolved to include more esoteric alcohols and ingredients, with a proclivity toward drawing out savory, surprising, and umami flavors in a drink, especially when in complement or contrast to the flavors of Jenny's food. The element of surprise in a drink is the ultimate goal for me. I love to watch guests' reactions

Photo credit: Dion Trinidad

as they sip something with certain expectations in mind but are led in a completely new direction by the flavor or texture. Some of my favorite experiments are with specialty syrups or vermouths I make from scratch, or obscure amaros and liqueurs I seek out for that certain je ne sais pas.

Nothing in life comes for free, and there are always trade-offs to making something "healthier." For me, the cocktails in this book are about keeping as much of the essence of a cocktail or the spirit of relaxing with a drink alive—but with subtle changes like reducing the alcohol an ounce, finding better sugar alternatives, mirroring complexity with natural flavorings instead of a prepackaged bottle. Living a healthy lifestyle is also about how the mind feels, and sometimes that means I do want to (and should) have that extra drink and gleefully order a dessert, too. Marathons and mixology are both part of my life, but neither one nor the other *are* my life—my "healthy" routine is as subject to ebbs and flows as is anyone else's, which may be fundamentally what makes us healthy and human. That's why I also incorporated some "Cheat Day" recipes in this book, because all things aside, I'm here to celebrate the spirit of what cocktail culture means to me: the joy of drinking something delicious, the candidness of interpersonal connection, and the enthusiasm to always be learning something new.

COCKTAILS 101

The jargon around cocktails was one of the first things I had to become comfortable with as a self-taught mixologist. I won't lie and say it was easy and that I picked things up seamlessly. There was absolutely a "ramp up" process, but as in any profession, building a foundation of knowledge is far more rewarding and useful in the long term than trying to "hack" your way into the cocktail world learning things piecemeal, or only one recipe at a time. Trust me, I tried the latter first—and I found I couldn't make any new drinks, only copy others, because I fundamentally didn't understand the *why* behind what I was doing. This chapter is a crash course in words, techniques, tools, and theories you should know before getting into making drinks. I believe once you're very comfortable being able to make high-quality, well-balanced regular-calorie cocktails, figuring out ways to "health-ify" them becomes a lot easier.

TOOLS

Shaker: An enclosed metal container with a base and a lid used to shake liquid cocktail ingredients, typically with ice and sometimes without (a *dry shake*). There are several types of shakers, notably, the *cobbler shaker*, a three-piece shaker that contains a base, lid with built-in strainer, and a cap that fits over the lid, and the *Boston shaker*, a two-part shaker with a metal base and a glass pint glass that fit tightly together (and that requires the use of a separate strainer).

Mixing Glass: Usually a glass beaker, but sometimes also a metal or container of a different material, that is used for stirred drinks. Ice is added to the mixing glass, alongside the cocktail ingredients, and the drink is stirred with a barspoon.

Jigger: An hourglass-shaped metal device that measures liquid cocktail ingredients. One side typically has a larger capacity than the other. Jiggers come in a variety of measurements, but I prefer jiggers that have a 1.5-ounce capacity on the large side and a 1-ounce capacity on the small side.

Strainers: There are three main types of strainers. The *Hawthorne*, often referred to simply as a cocktail strainer, has a metal spring that coils around a flat, perforated circular disc attached to a metal handle. The metal spring fits easily into standard cocktail shakers and mixing glasses and filters out the ice used for shaking the cocktail and other large particles. A *julep* strainer is a perforated concave metal disc with a handle. When inserted properly—at a slight angle—this fits snugly into shakers and mixing glasses to filter out ice and particles. A *chinois* or *fine-mesh strainer* is a cone-shaped strainer that is much finer in texture and that is often used as a second strainer for cocktails that require *double straining* through a Hawthorne and a fine mesh to remove smaller ice pieces or solid particles.

BlenderBottle: A brand of plastic shaking cups (most often used for protein shakes) that contains a wire ball to aerate the mixture. I started using these for egg white sours and flips after seeing the mixologists at Dead Rabbit—a cocktail bar in NYC that has consistently been named in the Top 5 of the world—using them behind the bar. I've found with the BlenderBottle, or other comparable shaking cups, you don't have to shake as vigorously to achieve a perfect texture and creamy consistency for great egg white sours and flips.

Barspoon: A long, thin metal spoon with a twisted stem and small spoon head (usually measuring roughly 1 teaspoon of liquid). The corkscrew ridges of the barspoon are used to pour streams of liquid into a glass without splashing, which is useful for layered drinks. The spoon head is used to *float* liquids on the top of cocktails by flipping the spoon upside down and gently pouring the liquid over the curved side.

Muddler: Similar in shape to a pestle, muddlers—often wood, plastic, or metal—are weighty cylindrical tubes used to mash, or "muddle," larger ingredients in a cocktail, such as whole fruits, for texture and flavor.

Ice: There are many different shapes and sizes of ice, usually corresponding with different styles of cocktails. While not always the case, you'll often find large *spherical ice* and *large square cubes* in spirit-forward, stirred drinks.

Collins ice is long and rectangular, slim enough to be inserted into a Collins or *highball* glass.

Cocktail ice, sometimes called to as *shaking ice*, refers to small square ice cubes used both in the shaker or mixer itself to chill and/or aerate the cocktail and as the ice served in the final glass. For any instances where cocktail ice is called for, those who have a standard ice tray or an ice-making function on their refrigerator can also substitute that rectangular ice for the square ice.

Crushed ice is small in size, like large ice pebbles. They are now usually prepared with a crushed-ice machine but can also be crushed less uniformly by using the back of a muddler. Crushed ice is most often found piled high on drinks like Moscow Mules or Mint Juleps to keep the drink cold and to bypass the issue of the smaller-sized ice melting too quickly and diluting the drink.

Pipette: A small plastic dropper used to carefully add specific doses of liquid ingredients to a cocktail. Pipettes serve the same purpose as glass *droppers*.

GLASSWARE

Collins / Highball: A cylindrical glass with straight walls, usually coming in a 12-ounce or 16-ounce size. Cocktails served in these glasses are usually shaken drinks that take a stack of cocktail ice or a stick of Collins ice.

Old-Fashioned / Tumbler: A stout glass that is much wider than a Collins, also with straight walls, typically in an 8-ounce size. This is the standard image that comes to mind when we envision a "stiff drink," but this glass is actually very versatile for shaken and stirred drinks, spirit-forward and non—you may find it used with a large glassy ice cube, or a trio of cocktail ice cubes, or something served neat.

Cocktail / Martini: A triangular stemmed glass best known for martinis with a spear of olive on the side. These glasses are also called, rather generically, "cocktail glasses" and generally contain shaken drinks served up.

Nick and Nora: Somewhat similar to the cocktail glass, this is also a stemmed glass but with a cuplike shape at top. These usually come in 4- to 5-ounce sizes and are also usually for drinks that are served up, both shaken and stirred.

Coupe: Another stemmed glass like the Nick and Nora, but with a much wider opening at the top so the shape looks more like a sideways bracket—like this }—than a cup. Coupes are generally a little larger in volume than Nick and Nora glasses, but are also used for cocktails served up that are shaken or stirred.

Tiki: Traditionally a ceramic vessel, but now sometimes also made of glass, these cylindrical vessels are much wider than a Collins and will have some sort of sculpture or carving on the façade. These are meant for tiki-style drinks, typically rum-based cocktails with "exotic" (i.e., tropically sourced) ingredients.

Mule: A standard mule glass is a copper mug with a handle, generally now lined on the interior with stainless steel to avoid any chemical reactions between the copper and acidic or dairy-based ingredients.

Flute: A tall, thin variation of a stemmed wineglass, generally used to serve sparkling wines like champagne. This is not often used for cocktails, but I find their dainty shape a nice variation for cocktails that would otherwise be served in a coupe or Nick and Nora. Because flutes were made to maintain as much effervescence of the liquid as possible, it's especially great for cocktails that have a fizzy component.

TERMINOLOGY

Up: When a beverage—either mixed or straight alcohol—is shaken or stirred with ice, then served cold in a glass without ice.

Neat: When an alcohol is served straight from the bottle to the glass, at room temperature with no ice.

On the Rocks: When a beverage—either mixed or straight alcohol—is served in a glass over ice.

Dry Shake: To shake all the ingredients inside of a cocktail shaker without ice.

Double Strain: To strain a cocktail through the cocktail strainer and a fine-mesh strainer into the glass. This is used for cocktails that have solid particles of varying sizes that may escape through the regular strainer.

Float: To layer a liquid ingredient on the top of a drink to create a visually layered effect. This requires the liquid being floated to be lighter (less dense) than the liquid it is being poured on top of to ensure it doesn't sink and mix into the cocktail. This is typically done by flipping a barspoon upside down, and gently pouring the floating liquid on the convex side of the spoon onto the top of the cocktail.

Express: To extract the essential oils from citrus rinds by squeezing the rind. I find one of the easiest ways to do this is to take a citrus peel and squeeze both ends in opposite directions. If you look carefully, you'll see a tiny spritz of oil being emitted from the peel; you can also then rub the peel against the sides of the cocktail glass to add more aromatics.

Rinse: To lightly coat the inside of the serving glass with a liquid ingredient and pour out the excess. This is meant to add just a hint of the taste of that ingredient to the final drink.

Dash: A somewhat loose measurement usually applied to cocktail bitters, based off of a flick of the wrist from the bottle. As a general rule of thumb, a dash is somewhere between approximately ⅛ and ⅕ of a teaspoon.

Sour: A family of cocktails that is composed of a base liquor, lemon or lime juice, and some type of sweetener. Famous examples are a whiskey sour or a sidecar. Egg whites are sometimes also added to contribute a foamy texture, much like a *flip*, but with minimal egg flavor.

Flip: A type of cocktail that now refers to the presence of a whole egg as one of the ingredients in the drink, in order to create a foamy top.

ABV: Alcohol By Volume is the amount of alcohol content (measured by ethanol) in an alcoholic spirit, written as a percentage of the total.

BASE RECIPES, SPECIALTY INGREDIENTS & BRANDS

SYRUPS

All of these syrups are made by combining the sweetener of choice with water in a small pot over low heat, and then stirring until the sweetener fully melts and integrates into the water. Let cool to room temperature before transferring to a food-safe container and storing in the refrigerator. These syrups are best used within one week, but can be made up to two weeks in advance.

Simple Syrup: A classic simple syrup is a ratio of 1 part water, 1 part sugar. Usually white table sugar is used, but you can also opt for a less-processed (but equally caloric) sugar such as raw cane sugar. The idea for all of the following syrups is to mimic the effect and sweetness of a regular simple syrup in a cocktail.

Honey Syrup: I use a ratio of 1.5 parts honey to 1 part water and stir until the honey has fully dissolved. I typically use clover honey, but you can also try varietals of honey like buckwheat for different colors and flavors. Honey is roughly twice as sweet as regular sugar, and I use a heavier ratio of honey in this syrup, so this is the only syrup that should be halved if being used in a recipe calling for "sweet syrup" but not explicitly for "honey syrup." While this syrup is still caloric, it is a more natural form of sweetness.

Xylitol Syrup: Xylitol is a sugar alcohol produced from raw materials such as birch wood and corn. It also occurs naturally in some plants and animals, including humans, and considered a natural product, although it has a rather off-putting, chemical-sounding name. Because xylitol is a sugar alcohol, it stimulates your taste buds to perceive the sensation of sweetness but contains far fewer calories (roughly 40 percent fewer) and does not raise blood sugar levels (on the glycemic index it ranks at 7, versus 60 to 70 for regular sugar). I use a 1:1 ratio of xylitol (which comes in crystallized form like white table sugar) to water for this syrup, same as the regular simple syrup, as it has a sweetness similar to that of table sugar. A note of caution to readers with pets: Xylitol is toxic to dogs and can have potentially life-threatening effects. As owners of two doggos ourselves, we encourage anyone with a dog to use extreme caution when bringing xylitol into your home. The safest choice is simply not to use it. But if you decide to use it (in preparing the recipes in this book or otherwise), please store it in a safe place away from your pets.

Monk Fruit Syrup: Monk fruit sugar is the dried juice of the monk fruit melon that is far, far sweeter than sugar (100 to 150 times sweeter) and has a glycemic index of 0. Because the sweet compounds within monk fruit are not absorbed by the body, we pass them through our systems completely, making monk fruit calorie free. Commercial monk fruit sugar is usually buffed up with other ingredients so it matches a sugar packet weight-wise (for the same sweetening power), so I generally use a 1:1 ratio of monk fruit to water for this syrup—but check your monk fruit sugar before you follow suit. If you have super pure monk fruit, you'll want to halve (if not quarter) the amount of monk fruit you use per serving of water to make this syrup.

Stevia: Stevia is a plant from the chrysanthemum family. Its leaves have a naturally sweet flavor. These leaves are then refined to make extracts such as rebaudioside A, a processed sweetener that is 200 times as sweet as regular sugar but contains no calories and has a glycemic index of 0 (just like monk fruit). Rebaudioside A is also the most common because it has the least bitterness of the various compounds available in the overall stevia leaf; many who do eat stevia will experience a metallic finish to their foods. If I do use stevia as a base for my syrups, I opt for a ratio of 1:4 stevia to water. I only use it for cocktails that have stronger ingredients that can help mask any potential lingering bitterness.

LIQUOR INFUSIONS

Cold Infusion: To infuse a base alcohol with another flavor without heating the spirit. This is done by combining the two ingredients and simply letting time do the work—infusions can take anywhere from a few hours to multiple weeks. This is usually best for delicate ingredients that can't be heated or would have their flavors impacted upon heating.

Hot Infusion: To infuse a base alcohol with another flavor by heating the two ingredients together. (Tea is, in its essence, a hot infusion.) This is much faster than cold infusions—typically only an hour or two—but is limited to hardier ingredients that can withstand hot temperatures. I will often use the sous vide method—keeping foods or ingredients in a certain temperature-controlled water bath—for hot infusions to better control the infusion temperature, minimize the heat impact on the flavoring ingredient and removing the need to boil the spirit (and lose some alcohol in the process).

For a basic hot infusion, combine your liquor base with what you're infusing it with in a nonreactive glass container and set your sous vide to 150°F (65.5°C). Test the flavor every hour to ensure it infuses to your desired level.

Milk / Fat Wash: To use the liquefied fat particles of dairy (like milk) or pure fat (like lard) to smooth the mouthfeel and tone down the alcoholic tinge of liquor.

For a basic milk punch or fat wash, liquefy your fat by heating it until melted or bringing milk to a light simmer. Combine immediately with your liquor base and you'll see the fat recongeal into beads or the milk curdle. Seal the container and shake vigorously—you'll see the fat or milk particles disperse into globules across the liquor and float to the top. Refrigerate the mixture and let it infuse for several hours, or even days, checking every 4 hours or so to see if it has reached your desired taste and texture. Once ready, carefully strain liquid through a fine-mesh strainer and cheesecloth or coffee filters. Note: For any liquors you've washed with milk or fat, make sure to keep them refrigerated and use within 2 weeks.

SPECIALTY INGREDIENTS

Xanthan Gum: A thickening and stabilizing agent often used as a food additive, produced through the fermentation of simple sugars. It is especially common to find xanthan in gluten-free baking products as well as sauces and dressings. I use xanthan primarily as a thickening agent in a few recipes, such as the Milk-Free Spiced Latte, to provide viscosity and a better mouthfeel.

Ms. Betters Bitters Miraculous Foamer: A specialty item that uses a secret proprietary blend of natural ingredients to re-create the foaming and emulsifying effect of egg whites but is completely vegan. You only need roughly ⅓ of a dropper to substitute for one large egg white.

ALCOHOLS

Like all things, a good cocktail starts with good ingredients. While I encourage everyone to use liquors they find enjoyable and are priced appropriately for them, I am often asked which brands I like to use for my drinks, so I've provided a short list of names I can count on for a good base liquor. Please do not see this list as exhaustive or restrictive but simply as a good starting point if you are at the liquor store and unsure of where to start with the many options available.

Gin

London Dry:
- Tanqueray
- Hendricks

Old Tom:
- Ransom
- Hayman's

Vodka
- Tito's
- Reyka
- St George

Bourbon
- Four Roses
- Elijah Craig
- Basil Hayden's

Rye
- Bulleit
- Redemption
- Woodford Reserve

Scotch

Blended
- Famous Grouse
- Monkey Shoulder

Single Malt
- Glenlivet (Speyside)
- Laphroaig (Islay)
- Glenmorangie (Highlands)
- Oban (Highlands)
- Springbank (Campbeltown)

Rum
- Sailor Jerry's (Spiced)
- Flor de Caña
- Diplomático

Tequila/Mezcal
- Espolon
- Herradura
- Del Maguey (Mezcal)

Vermouth (Sweet & Dry)
- Dolin
- Noilly Prat

VODKA & GIN

VODKA

Vodka is often seen as the quintessentially "healthy" alcohol, though another spirit actually claims the prize (more on that later!). Distilled from a limitless number of different ingredients —traditionally cereal grains or potato—the main standard for vodka is that it is exceedingly clean and neutral, ready to take on any flavor you give it.

Vodka's strength as a blending liquor really shines when used to showcase bright, refreshing drinks, especially when more subtly flavored fruits, vegetables, or herbs are present. I think about summer barbeques, basking in the warm sun with a zesty cooler in hand, or a casual Sunday brunch, sipping a Bloody Mary with a juicy olive. One of vodka's best qualities is its penchant for a range of infusions, like caraway-flavored aquavit from Scandinavia or sweet, lemon-scented *limoncello* from Italy—both easy to make with a foundation of quality vodka. I urge you to experiment with your favorite fruits and vegetables to add extra relish to cocktails without additional calories.

Bone Broth Bloody "Bull"

No brunch is complete without a savory Bloody Mary, especially when it's tomato season. Like most, the Dorsey household has seen our fill of two-toned Bloody Marys made of V8 and well vodka, sometimes seasoned with a salt-laden beef bouillon. So, this seemed a perfect opportunity for me to help others break out of that mold and showcase the height of summer produce while fortifying the drink with deep, complex, collagen-rich bone broth. There's a vibrancy and depth in this Bloody I find hard to match: fresh tomatoes offer an irreplaceable brightness and acid, fish sauce lends another layer of umami to the otherwise neutral vodka base, and aromatics like celery salt (the secret of why Old Bay is so good) and Sichuan peppercorn (a floral spice that leaves tingly afternotes) tie everything together. This is a drink that's anything but mundane, and it deserves a place at the table even after the food has been cleared away. Spice it up with your favorite hot sauce for a personal touch; I love the robust chili crisps from Lao Gan Ma brand (available online or in most Asian grocery markets) or a garlicky sambal. In my household, I garnish with a celery heart, cornichons, and pearl onions on a skewer and a generous dusting of bacon salt (crispy bacon ground with kosher salt and black pepper) but, by all means, your Bloody, your way.

INGREDIENTS

Bloody Bull Mix

2 cups fresh tomato puree

2 cups fire-roasted, crushed, canned tomatoes

1¼ cups unsalted bone broth (I use homemade beef broth, but Kettle & Fire or Pacific Foods are good prepackaged choices)

2½ ounces fresh lime juice

2 ounces fish sauce (I use Red Boat brand 40°N)

15 whole Sichuan peppercorns

1½ tablespoons sweet syrup

Kosher salt, as needed

Celery salt, as needed

Per Bloody Bull

2 ounces vodka

6 ounces Bloody Bull mix

INSTRUCTIONS

1. Puree all ingredients for Bloody Bull mix in blender until smooth. Season with salt and celery salt to taste.

2. Combine vodka and Bloody Bull mix in shaker with ice. Shake and pour over ice in a Collins glass.

3. Garnish as desired.

Cilantro Celery Collins

This is a fun one! Cilantro is a staple ingredient in the kind of food the two of us regularly eat at home, and I've always been enamored with how much structure even a small amount of cilantro can lend to a dish. Because it's so herbaceous and enjoyably bitter, I've found it to be very useful as a stand-in for drinks that would otherwise rely on amaros, which I also adore (I am half Italian, so you could say amaros are in my blood) *but* unfortunately tend to contain a lot of sugar. This drink is meant for those who like savory, aromatic flavors with the combination of celery, cilantro, and lime for a dazzling green and vegetable-forward finish.

INGREDIENTS

1½ ounces vodka
1¼ ounces celery juice
¼ ounce cilantro, juiced
½ ounce lime juice
¾ ounce sweet syrup
2 ounces sparkling water

INSTRUCTIONS

1. Combine vodka, celery juice, cilantro juice, lime juice, and sweet syrup in shaker with ice.

2. Shake vigorously and double strain into a Collins glass.

3. Top with sparkling water and stir lightly.

Note: If you do not have a juicer, you can blend the celery and cilantro in a blender on high, then strain through a cheesecloth to catch the juice.

Beets & Basil

Every week, I eat an almost embarrassing amount of root vegetables. It's one of my favorite vegetable categories: simple to prepare (I poke and roast, then top with salt and pepper) and fills me up even when I'm constantly hungry from marathon training. My main staple these days is spaghetti squash, as it's a little lower in sugar and the least aggravating to peel, but if I want to really "treat myself," I'll always go for beets. Unlike my wife, who despises beets ("they taste like dirt," she says), I find them to be just the right amount of earthy and sweet. In this cocktail, the beet juice introduces all the sugar needed in the drink while providing a savory backbone that lifts the balsamic vinegar, while the basil provides that lovely top note so reminiscent of a good salad.

INGREDIENTS

6 basil leaves
½ ounce lemon juice
1½ ounces vodka
2 ounces red beet juice
1 barspoon high-quality
  balsamic vinegar
1 pinch salt

INSTRUCTIONS

1. Muddle basil leaves with lemon juice in shaker.

2. Add vodka, beet juice, balsamic vinegar, salt, and ice.

3. Shake vigorously and double strain into a coupe or Nick and Nora glass.

Moscow Mule

The Moscow Mule is an iconic drink served in a copper mug, which has now colloquially taken on the name "mule mug." Its origins are slightly unclear, but the trio of flavors—vodka, ginger, lime—has always been consistent. To keep the spirit of the mule alive but significantly reduce the sugar content, which stems from the ginger beer, I muddle fresh ginger for a spicy kick and top it off with sparkling water for effervescence. Since a good-quality ginger beer has a certain bite to it that can't be replicated by just fresh ginger, I also add a dash of bitters to the sparkling water. (I find this could also be replicated using tonic water, which contains quinine, but because tonic water is rather caloric, the bitters/sparkling water combination is very close and much healthier.) It's certainly not an exact replica, but I think you'll find this version extremely fresh and enjoyable both in cold and hot months. If you love all things spicy like me, add double the amount of ginger.

INGREDIENTS

3 (⅛-inch-thick) slices
    ginger, peeled
½ ounce fresh lime juice
2 ounces vodka
½ ounce sweet syrup
2 dashes Angostura bitters
3 ounces sparkling water
1 lime wedge, for garnish

INSTRUCTIONS

1. Muddle ginger with lime juice in a shaker.

2. Add vodka, sweet syrup, bitters, and ice.

3. Shake vigorously and double strain into a Collins glass with ice.

4. Top with sparkling water and stir gently. Garnish.

Pumpkin Matcha Fizz

My wife Jenny grew up eating salted, roasted pumpkin seeds dusted in green tea—it's a ubiquitous snack among the Chinese community, and you'll find it at almost any gathering to nibble on before dinner, after dinner, over some beverages, or propped up watching TV. It's so commonplace to her, she never bothered to introduce me to them until recently, when we were buying snacks for a cocktail hour we were hosting for our nonprofit. I grabbed a handful of them and ate them whole, much to Jenny's shock. "You're supposed to shell them!" she told me. Well, let me just say these seeds are so well seasoned, you probably won't mind the shells (plus, it adds some crunch). This cocktail is a fun play on the flavors of these snacks, which are both nutritionally sound, too: matcha is premium green tea powder full of antioxidants and chlorophyll (a detoxifier) while pumpkin seeds offer plenty of healthy fat.

INGREDIENTS

1½ ounces vodka
½ teaspoon matcha powder
3 ounces cold water
¼ teaspoon pumpkin seed oil
1 egg white *or* ⅓ of a dropper (approximately 3 milliliters) Ms. Bitters Miraculous Foamer
½ ounce sweet syrup
Sparkling water, as needed
Matcha powder, for garnish

INSTRUCTIONS

1. Combine vodka, matcha powder, water, pumpkin seed oil, egg white (or Miraculous Foamer), and sweet syrup in BlenderBottle with ice.

2. Shake vigorously and strain into Collins glass with ice.

3. Top with soda water until the foam rises above the rim of the glass.

4. Garnish with matcha powder.

Saved by the Bell

I'm not completely sure when this recipe happened—I think I was at home, grazing through the refrigerator (as I do every hour or so), and felt the inclination to make a new drink. We often have a lot of leftover green bell peppers, as one of Jenny's signature sauces—habanero chutney—requires mounds and mounds of tiny green bell pepper dice. Dill is another ingredient we love, especially with lamb, and, surprisingly, these two strong vegetable flavors also work well together without fighting each other. It's basically green juice, right?

Oh, and growing up, I was completely obsessed with the sitcom *Saved by the Bell*, so I couldn't help but give a nod to this classic with the name of this drink.

INGREDIENTS

3–4 fresh dill sprigs
½ ounce fresh lime juice
1½ ounces vodka
1 ounce fresh green bell
    pepper juice
½ ounce sweet syrup

INSTRUCTIONS

1. Muddle dill sprigs with lime juice in shaker.

2. Add remaining ingredients to shaker with ice.

3. Shake vigorously and double strain into Collins glass with ice.

A-"Pear"-itif

I love Asian pears. They are so succulent, yet hearty enough to keep me full between meals (which is not an easy feat for a runner!). Paired with shiso, an aromatic, citrusy leaf common in Japanese and Korean cooking, this drink makes for a delicate aperitif or top-of-the-evening drink. There's even a touch of caffeine from mild white tea to help you get ready for dinner.

INGREDIENTS

2–3 shiso leaves (or spearmint if shiso is unavailable)
½ ounce lemon juice
1½ ounces vodka
2 ounces Asian pear juice
½ ounce white tea
½ sweet syrup

INSTRUCTIONS

1. Muddle shiso leaves with lemon juice in shaker.

2. Add remaining ingredients with ice.

3. Shake vigorously and double strain into cocktail glass or coupe.

GIN

Gin is for the botanical enthusiastic who loves the smell of herbs and spices and its hearty zippiness in a beverage. The most characteristic quality of gin is the presence of juniper berries, the round berry of a cold-weather tree with a distinctive woody sharpness and just a touch of sweetness. Gin and juniper are so closely tied, the word *gin* is actually the abbreviated version of *genever*, or Dutch for "juniper" (not to be confused with the Dutch Jenever liquor—sometimes also spelled Genever—the national beverage that also tastes similar to gin but sweeter). Like vodka, gin is made from a neutral, distilled spirit—typically made from grains—but the difference is that gin is distilled with herbal and spice additions like juniper, wormwood, and coriander. (In a pinch, you could make your own gin by infusing vodka with a similar mix of botanicals.) In recent years, gin has seen somewhat of a craft revival, with smaller, local distilleries all putting their own spin on the flavoring blend. St. George in Alameda, California, uses Douglas fir for theirs; the selling point for Hendricks has always been their inclusion of rose and cucumber. Some differences are more wildly pronounced than others, so we always encourage you to take a sip of a new gin before using it in a cocktail.

When most of us talk about gin, the variety that comes to mind is London Dry. This is the most common version of gin and specifically entails a clear, unsweetened liquid distilled from an agricultural (or plant-based) ingredient with no added or artificial flavorings that is infused during the distillation process and not afterward. This is a very pure, straight version with enough structure to hold up to bold flavors without masking them. Another variety, Old Tom, is a classic style of gin from the eighteenth century with a rounder, sweeter touch. It has become a craft favorite, dry but slightly less intense, with a softer alcoholic bite. I like Old Tom for flavors that are herbaceous and green but delicate enough to warrant a lighter partner. While the brands Ransom and Hayman's are fairly well distributed, Old Tom gin can admittedly be tough to find and is typically more expensive than London Dry. A third style of gin, Plymouth, is a staple in classic cocktail books like the *Savoy Cocktail Book*, but is only produced by one distillery: Plymouth. It's drier, more citrus forward, and tends to be a bit spicier than London Dry, making it a good match for more bitter cocktails like the Negroni. The final gin is not exactly a gin, but a liqueur, a distilled spirit sweetened with various oils, extracts, or flavors after distillation. *Sloe gin* is far sweeter than its counterparts, from the combination of gin with sloe (a sour, astringent stone fruit common in England). The result is tart, sugary, and rich. While I appreciate sloe gin and find it has useful applications in cocktails, I have avoided using it in this book due to its high sugar content.

Eat Your Peas!

I love snap peas. I eat them all the time—plain and raw, with a scoop of hummus, in a quick sauté with garlic and lime, sliced thin in a salad with dill and tarragon. My favorite part is the satisfying snap when biting into one, releasing that distinctly green, vegetable sweetness reminiscent of warm months. This cocktail is meant to evoke the essence of salad in a glass: refreshing, bright, a little floral, and all-around a feel-good beverage. The use of Old Tom here allows the demure qualities of snap peas to really stand out, while providing a supple mouthfeel and adding some body to the otherwise airy note of tarragon. There's a lot more snap pea in this drink than you might think—that's what preserves the lively green, which is so eye-catching even non–gin drinkers may be tempted to try it. Garnishing with a snap pea on the half-shell completes the look, though be warned: finding peas with a row of bulbous pods may be more challenging than it probably should be (the good news is any discards make for excellent eating!).

INGREDIENTS

4 sugar snap pea pods
8–10 tarragon leaves
¾ ounce sweet syrup
2 ounces Old Tom gin
½ ounce dry vermouth

INSTRUCTIONS

1. Muddle snap pea pods, tarragon, and simple syrup in a cocktail shaker.

2. Add gin and vermouth with ice.

3. Shake vigorously and double strain into Old-Fashioned glass filled with crushed ice or a large ice cube.

4. Garnish with sugar snap pea pod, if desired.

Gotham Sunset

Manhattanhenge is a big, *big* deal in New York City. A few times each year around the summer solstice, the sunset and sunrise align with the street grid of Manhattan and pedestrians are treated to a glowing display of nature and human-built creation briefly working as one. I'd heard about this occurrence for years, but like most busy New Yorkers, I always seemed to miss it, complain forlornly afterward, and forget all about it until it passed me by again. But one serendipitous day, I happened to leave the office of my former company at just the right time. We were located on Twenty-Third Street, coincidentally one of the best viewing locations, and I was stopped in my tracks by the glow of a deeply orange sun, transforming the ordinary streets of taxis, people, and delivery bicycles into something magical.

I wanted to evoke that feeling, the beauty of that view, in this cocktail. To capture the brilliance of color, stunning even from afar, and the unexpected surprise upon first sip. Carrot juice gives this drink that vibrant color, while being slightly heavier to balance out the intensity and directness of London Dry gin. Orange blossom water (a by-product of bitter orange oil production) is a specialty ingredient, popular in the Middle East for its distinctive perfume, but I promise it's well worth finding—it's this floral top note that really gives the cocktail its breakthrough uniqueness. I named this drink the Gotham Sunset, as I like to think this is a beverage anyone would want to drink while watching a really beautiful sunset.

INGREDIENTS

1½ ounces London Dry gin
1½ ounces fresh carrot juice
1 ounce fresh orange juice
¾ ounce sweet syrup
½ ounce fresh lemon juice
3–4 drops orange blossom water*

INSTRUCTIONS

1. Combine all ingredients over ice and shake.

2. Pour into Old-Fashioned glass with a large ice cube.

3. Garnish with an orange blossom flower, if desired.

---

* Orange blossom water is available at most liquor stores as well as in the specialty or global section of many grocery stores.

Raspberry Sour

I made this drink shortly after we moved to San Francisco. We packed up our lives, including one large dog, and drove across the country in the middle of the summer. When we arrived, we were welcomed with blustery wind and cloudy skies—unknown to us, the Bay Area is known for cool summers and frequent "Indian summers," unseasonably dry, warm weather in the fall. Barbeque season was not in full swing until November, so when it did come, we were out in full force, shish kebabs and foil-wrapped corn at the ready. I remember we were preparing for our first BBQ meetup with friends, and I wanted to make something special for everyone to enjoy as we waited for the grill.

Raspberries are particularly plump and lovely in San Francisco—they thrive in cool, coastal conditions—and I naturally gravitated toward their distinguishing sweet-tart taste and pink hue. The addition of egg white makes it a sour-style cocktail, giving it a lovely foam top while toning down the pucker of raspberry. I especially like Hendricks for this drink because the subtle rose and cucumber notes complements the berry and keeps the cocktail from being overly fruity and predictable.

INGREDIENTS

7 large raspberries
½ ounce fresh lemon juice
1½ ounces gin
½ ounce sweet syrup
1 egg white *or* ⅓ of a
    dropper (approximately
    3 milliliters) Ms. Bitters
    Miraculous Foamer

INSTRUCTIONS

1. Muddle raspberries with lemon juice in BlenderBottle.

2. Add gin, sweet syrup, egg white (or Miraculous Foamer) with ice.

3. Shake vigorously and double strain into coupe.

4. Garnish with a spear of raspberries, if desired.

Spicy Bee's Knees

Bee's Knees is a classic gin cocktail that should be in every mixologist's repertoire. It's already made with honey, so I naturally thought of adding some cayenne to bump up the spiciness, as those two ingredients pair so well together. This is an easy-drinking beverage that will help clear out your sinuses, and it serves as a nice digestif after a good meal.

INGREDIENTS

2 ounces London Dry gin
¾ ounce fresh lemon juice
½ ounce honey syrup (I use clover honey)*
1 pinch ground cayenne pepper, for garnish

INSTRUCTIONS

1. Combine gin, lemon juice, and honey syrup in shaker with ice.

2. Shake vigorously and strain into a chilled cocktail or Nick and Nora glass.

3. Garnish with a pinch of cayenne pepper.

*For a more savory version of this, add a few cloves of garlic while your honey syrup infuses for a garlicky honey that helps fight colds and also tastes great with cayenne.

Beer's Knees

A shandy (a cocktail made with beer) is often touted as a good hangover cure, but mixing alcohols has never made me feel particularly good afterward. In this rendition, I replace the beer with a lightly carbonated kombucha, which adds the fizz of a summer shandy while promoting the healthy bacteria in our guts.

INGREDIENTS

3–4 lemon wedges, for garnish
2 ounces London Dry gin
¾ ounce lemon juice
½ ounce honey syrup
3 ounces ginger-flavored kombucha

INSTRUCTIONS

1. Fill Collins glass with ice and lemon wedges.

2. Combine gin, lemon juice, and honey syrup in shaker with ice.

3. Shake vigorously and strain into Collins glass.

4. Top with ginger kombucha.

Tom Collins

The Tom Collins is a simple gin cocktail that is quite forgiving—it almost always tastes good—and serves as ripe ground to build up confidence as you're experimenting. Try replacing the sweet syrup with other natural sweeteners like muddled fruit, or switching lemon juice for lime and adding your own mix of botanicals, herbs, or spices.

INGREDIENTS

2 ounces London Dry gin
1 ounce lemon juice
½ ounce sweet syrup
1 ounce soda water

INSTRUCTIONS

1. Combine London Dry gin, lemon juice, and sweet syrup in Collins glass with ice

2. Stir until the outside of the glass becomes cold.

3. Top with soda water.

Isle of Capri

My mother's half of the family are true Italian Americans. Originally hailing from Sicily, they settled on New York's Arthur Avenue for a generation before dispersing to Brooklyn, then the Midwest, and finally "fleeing the cold" (as my mother puts it) to South Carolina and South Florida for some sun. Nani Jo, my great-grandmother, was well known in her day for packing up balls and balls of freshly pulled mozzarella from her neighborhood cheesemonger in NYC and taking it with her on a bus to Folly Beach, a beachy area outside Charleston where my grandmother Nani Ro now lives. Naturally, the cheese was beyond melted after the daylong journey, but somehow the caprese salads Nani Jo made for us at family gatherings were still outstanding. Nani Jo has since passed (at the age of 101! Nani Ro is 92 as of this writing!), but this cocktail, which is "caprese in a glass," lives on to celebrate their lives as strong Italian women who both had a part in raising me.

INGREDIENTS

2 Italian basil leaves
½ ounce lemon juice
1½ ounces gin
1 ounce tomato water* (preferably from heirloom tomatoes)
½ ounce sweet syrup
¼ ounce balsamic vinegar
1 basil leaf, for garnish
3–5 drops extra virgin olive oil, for garnish

INSTRUCTIONS

1. Muddle two basil leaves with lemon juice in shaker.

2. Add gin, tomato water, sweet syrup, and balsamic vinegar with ice.

3. Shake vigorously and double strain into Old-Fashioned glass with large ice cube.

4. Garnish with basil leaf and extra virgin olive oil.

Note: When garnishing with fresh herbs, lay the herb flat in one hand and clap your hands lightly to release the aromatics.

*Tomato water is simply pureed tomatoes that have been strained to remove the solids.

Cheat Day Challenge!
Ramos Gin Fizz

The Ramos Gin Fizz is a famous cocktail hailing from New Orleans, created by Henry C. Ramos. It's decidedly not a "healthy" drink, with its indulgent creaminess (heavy cream and egg white) and a floral note of orange blossom. However, it's a cocktail that truly opened my eyes to the possibilities of egg whites breathing new life into a cocktail, and I think it's something anyone serious about mixology should make a few times to simply marvel at. As our first **Cheat Day Challenge**, here's my version of a Ramos Gin Fizz for when you want to treat yourself. If you would prefer to make it dairy free, you can replace heavy cream with a heavier nut milk (such as coconut, oat, or cashew) whizzed with a bit of xanthan gum, but that will, of course, change the flavor of the drink. If you want to make it completely vegan, you can also replace the egg white with Miraculous Foamer.

INGREDIENTS

2 ounces London Dry gin

1 ounce heavy cream

½ ounce lime juice

½ ounce lemon juice

2 teaspoons sweet syrup

2–3 drops orange blossom water*

1 egg white**

2 ounces sparkling water

INSTRUCTIONS

1. Combine gin, cream, lime juice, lemon juice, sweet syrup, orange blossom water, and egg white in BlenderBottle.

2. Dry shake (without ice) vigorously for 20 seconds.

3. Add ice to BlenderBottle and shake vigorously for an additional 20 seconds.

(Continued on next page)

4. Double strain into Collins glass and place in refrigerator for 2 to 3 minutes.

5. Remove from refrigerator and, using a straw, poke a hole in the center of the foam at the top of the drink.

6. Slowly pour sparkling water into the hole until the foam rises above the rim of the glass.

---

*Orange blossom water is available at most liquor stores as well as in the specialty or global section of many grocery stores.

**If you are nervous about using fresh egg whites, you can always pasteurize them before use. To pasteurize large eggs, cook them gently at temperatures between 140°F to 142°F for 3 minutes before shocking in ice water. Use as you would regular raw eggs. (Note: This doesn't completely eliminate any possibility of salmonella, but it's a good precaution.)

WHISK(E)YS

Whisk(e)y is a big and often not well-understood category, starting with how it's spelled. In general, the difference in spelling indicates where the whisk(e)y was made. For those from Ireland or the United States, the alcohol is referred to as "whiskey," while all other countries drop the "e" and spell it "whisky."

The widest catch-all definition for whisk(e)y is a distilled alcohol made from the mash of fermented grains. There is a seemingly endless number of types of whisk(e)y, varying based on the grain, geography, and production method, but some of the more common subcategories are

- *Bourbon*—American whiskey made from 51–80 percent corn, aged in new, charred American white-oak barrels
- *Scotch*—the generic term for whisky made in Scotland. Scotch has many subcategories based on geography, including Speyside, Highlands, or Islay, that are distinguished by the flavor profiles characterizing each region.
- *Rye*—made from at least 51 percent rye aged in new, charred American oak barrels
- *White*—known colloquially as *moonshine*, white, or unaged, whiskey is bottled directly after distillation, typically with the addition of water to lower the ABV. White whiskey has risen in popularity in recent years, particularly those offerings that infuse the liquor with fresh fruit like cherries, peaches, or spiced apples.

- *Malted*—made from at least 51 percent malted barley. A *single malt* is a malt whisk(e)y made from a single distillery. While the term *single malt* is most often associated with Scotch, the term can be used for any malt whisk(e)y produced from a single distillery regardless of the location.
- *Blended*—refers to a mixture of different kinds of whisk(e)y

Compared to vodka and gin, whisk(e)y gives a much deeper, richer taste and body to cocktails and a specific alcoholic taste to the overall makeup of the drink. The way I see it, whisk(e)y is not a base spirit meant to be masked in a cocktail; it should be chosen to complement and build on the other ingredients. Each whisk(e)y offers something unique, depending on how the grain mixture is treated and in what barrel and for how long the liquid is aged. For example, the ultra-smoky Scotch some love is from the use of peat smoke in the malting process. Bourbon is often described as caramel-y and coconutty because it is aged in new, American charred oak barrels which are known for compounds that release a signature coconutty and dill scent (which will often also be mentioned in wines aged in American oak).

Everyone has their own whisk(e)y of choice, so while I have separated this chapter of cocktail recipes by category of whisk(e)y, they are certainly not set in stone. As you begin to try different kinds of whisk(e)y and find your natural preference, feel free to swap out one style for another to see how the composition of the drink changes. The only caveat I'll make here is that super-premium, high-end whisk(e)ys are generally meant for drinking alone, versus mixed in a cocktail, but that is also up to your discretion (and wallet!).

BOURBON

Relative to other whiskies, bourbon offers a sweeter lift to cocktails, with notes of chewy toffee, vanilla, and caramel. It's one of the more rounded forms of whisk(e)y, with a noticeably lighter alcohol burn in my opinion, and works well for drinks that need a stronger foundation. Bourbon isn't so forward that it steals the spotlight from the other flavors, such as fruit and spice, that may be present in a drink.

Although bourbon is produced throughout the United States, an overwhelming majority is produced in Kentucky, and the spirit is strongly associated with Kentucky and the southern United States more broadly. While we won't go into the rich and detailed history of the spirit here, one interesting distinction worth pointing out is the subcategory Tennessee whiskey (made famous by its most popular brands, Jack Daniels and George Dickel). The makers of Tennessee whiskey distinguish themselves from bourbon produced in other parts of the country through a process by which unaged whiskey is filtered through sugar maple wood charcoal before going into the barrel to age (known as the Lincoln County Process). The makers of Tennessee whiskey claim that the process makes their whiskey smoother than other bourbons. While it still technically meets the legal requirements of bourbon, the spirit is labeled distinctly as Tennessee whiskey.

The recipes that follow don't call for a specific type of bourbon, so choose whichever you prefer!

Mint Julep

I grew up in South Florida, but I spent much of my young adult life in the Southern heartland. I went to school in North Carolina and then moved to Atlanta for five years for my first two jobs. In the South, one of the biggest events of the summer is undoubtedly the Kentucky Derby. No matter what your age, profession, or stage of life, if you liked horse racing or not at all, the Derby was always an exciting springtime extravaganza of seersucker suits and big hats. When I come across my old Derby photos now, I laugh at the ridiculous outfits I once decided were posh enough to sport all day, but I do have some great memories of the event throughout the years: relaxing with old friends and meeting new ones, indulging in a litany of bright cocktails like Mint Juleps, Blackberry Smash, Pimm's Cup, and Brown Derby. Even though I'm now a full-time New Yorker heading to the Belmont Stakes to watch the occasional horse race, sipping on some of these Southern classics somehow always makes the event more enjoyable. Since the originals are often laden with sugar and syrups, I've lightened up the Mint Julep and Blackberry Smash with a sugar alternative and included the Brown Derby in its natural form (a surprisingly already-healthy classic).

INGREDIENTS

8–10 mint leaves
¼ ounce sweet syrup
2 ounces bourbon
1 mint sprig, for garnish

INSTRUCTIONS

1. Muddle mint leaves with sweet syrup directly in serving glass.
2. Add bourbon and sweet syrup–mint mixture to cup and pack with cubed or crushed ice.
3. Stir drink in glass until glass is cold on the outside.
4. If necessary, add more ice so that cubes or crushed ice rise above the rim of the glass.
5. Garnish with a mint sprig and serve. For a sweet treat, dust the top with powdered sugar!

Note: Mint Juleps are typically served in a stainless steel or copper julep cup. If you have these, then great! But a set of these can get a bit pricey, so an Old-Fashioned glass also works great.

Southern Blessing

Peach season is a big deal in Georgia and South Carolina (little-known secret: the best peaches are from South Carolina, not the "Peach State" of Georgia). Every May, I remember my mother would always receive a box of freshly picked peaches from her client in South Carolina—fuzzy, ripe and juicy, straight from his backyard trees. I had to be forcibly withheld from the peaches to ensure the rest of my family could also have some peaches to eat, but I usually ate the vast majority of the box anyway. This cocktail is more or less an excuse for me to buy loads of peaches when the weather warms up and peaches start coming up north; if you want to make it extra special, grill the peaches before juicing for a satisfying charred flavor.

INGREDIENTS

3 ounces peach juice
1½ ounces bourbon
¼ ounce sweet syrup
2 dashes aromatic bitters
Pinch each of ground
    cinnamon, ground
    clove, ground nutmeg,
    for garnish
Cinnamon stick, for
    garnish

INSTRUCTIONS

1. Fill a mug with boiling water and let stand for a minute or two to warm.

2. Warm peach juice, bourbon, sweet syrup, and bitters on stove to just under a boil.

3. Empty the water from the mug and replace with warm peach juice/bourbon mixture.

4. Top with ground spices and garnish with cinnamon stick.

Blackberry Smash

The smash is a category of cocktails intended to highlight the freshest and brightest fruits of any given season. While the technical definition of what makes a smash a smash is up for debate, the cocktail is typically composed of a combination of muddled fruit, herbs, and a base spirit. Muddle the fruit directly in the glass for a chunky, pulpy expression or strain it out for a smooth, clean sipper. Infuse your spirit with herbs, muddle them alongside the fruit, or simply use them as a garnish; the choice is all yours. As for the spirit, I find that bourbon works well with sweeter fruits like berries or stone fruit. For more sour fruits like kiwi or passion fruit, rum or a floral spirit such as gin is great. With a set of "rules" like that, you're free to make a cocktail that suits any occasion.

INGREDIENTS

6 blackberries
5 large mint leaves
¾ ounce sweet syrup
2½ ounces bourbon
3 blackberries, for garnish
2 mint leaves, for garnish

INSTRUCTIONS

1. Muddle blackberries, mint, and sweet syrup in cocktail shaker.

2. Add bourbon and ice.

3. Shake vigorously and double strain into Old-Fashioned glass with large square ice cube.

4. Garnish with spear of blackberries and mint leaves, if desired.

Brown Derby

With a name like the Brown Derby, it's easy to think that this drink finds its roots in the stables of Churchill Downs. Interestingly enough, however, the drink originates from the glitz and glamour of 1930s Hollywood and is named for a restaurant in Los Angeles that was literally shaped like a derby hat. Despite its coastal beginnings, this drink has found its way onto menus across the country and is a favorite summertime refresher no matter where you are.

INGREDIENTS

1½ ounces bourbon
1 ounce grapefruit juice
½ ounce honey syrup

INSTRUCTIONS

1. Add all ingredients to shaker with ice.

2. Shake vigorously and strain into coupe.

Eggless Cold Brew Flip

A well-made cold brew is truly one of life's great little pleasures. Ever since cold brew burst onto the scene years ago, I've almost all but switched up my coffee consumption to only cold brew. (The name "cold brew" can be misleading—it is brewed cold, as in the coffee grounds are not heated to extract flavor, but the final product can absolutely be served hot!) I personally am one of those people who can drink caffeine at any hour and have no trouble sleeping, so enjoying cold brew during happy hour and beyond has been nothing short of a call to action for me. This is an ultrasimple coffee cocktail that can serve as the base for many variations: a flavored syrup, perhaps, or a blend of different whiskeys, even some vanilla or peppermint extract to liven it up. The Miraculous Foamer takes the place of an egg to make this drink creamy, with a gorgeous cappuccino-like foam cap that transitions easily from coffeehouse to cocktail bar.

INGREDIENTS

1½ ounce bourbon
2 ounces cold brew coffee concentrate
½ ounce sweet syrup
⅓ dropper Ms. Betters Bitters Miraculous Foamer

INSTRUCTIONS

1. Combine all ingredients in a BlenderBottle with ice.

2. Shake vigorously for 30 seconds.

3. Strain into a coupe or Nick and Nora glass.

Green & Black

On one of our early dates back in 2013, Jenny and I went to the rooftop of the Metropolitan Museum of Art in NYC. The rooftop of the museum is a not-so-secret gem amid the Upper East Side landscape, only open on sunny days during the summer, offering glorious views clear across Central Park to the iconic buildings of New York. I was still new to the city then, and I remember being perched against the railing, enjoying the warm breeze as Jenny tried out the panorama function of her iPhone (that was a new thing back then!). There was one drink at the upstairs cocktail bar I ordered, something along the lines of a Cardamom Bourbon Punch, and it was so good, I decided to re-create it when we returned home. It was the very first cocktail I ever made without relying on any recipe template online—a proud point of my journey as a self-trained mixologist. It's withstood my scrutiny over the years, and I think you'll find it simple to make yet subtle and refined.

INGREDIENTS

5 green cardamom pods
½ ounce sweet syrup
1½ ounces bourbon
1½ ounces English
    breakfast tea, chilled
2 green cardamom pods,
    crushed gently by palm,
    for garnish

INSTRUCTIONS

1. Muddle cardamom pods with sweet syrup in shaker.

2. Add bourbon, tea, and ice.

3. Shake vigorously and double strain into Old-Fashioned glass with large square ice cube.

4. Garnish with green cardamom pods.

Note: Green cardamom can be pricey, but a little goes a long way, and the flavor simply cannot be replaced by other types of spices. To gently crush the pods to release the most of their goodness, use the palm of your hand to crack open the outside green shell.

Cheat Day Challenge!
Five-Spice Old-Fashioned

Five-spice powder—a mixture of Sichuan peppercorn, star anise, cinnamon, fennel seeds, and clove—is a staple of Chinese food and a smell and taste I've now come to associate with home. When pork belly was the hottest thing in food, and every client under the sun would request it for our events, Jenny would make this absurdly tender, stewed version with tons of freshly made five-spice powder. I may or may not have gorged myself on several literal pounds of it one night and fallen asleep with my clothes still on, but I digress. This cocktail is a challenge recipe because it requires fat-washing, but I think once you do your first fat-wash, you'll fall in love with how effective and easy it is. I use Chinese sausage, a pork sausage that is both sweet and savory, to soften and add layers of meaty umami to the bourbon. It's available at most Asian grocery stores near the pork products or online, and it really does make this drink a cut above the standard Old-Fashioned.

INGREDIENTS

2 ounces Chinese sausage fat-washed bourbon* (I use Kam Yen Jan brand)

½ ounce five-spice sweet syrup**

2–3 dashes Angostura bitters

1 star anise pod, for garnish

Note: Star anise has a specific licorice-y flavor that serves as an excellent mouth freshener. Just chew on one of the points after your drink to refresh your palate!

INSTRUCTIONS

1. Combine bourbon, five-spice syrup, and Angostura bitters with ice in mixing glass.

2. Stir continuously for 30 seconds to mix thoroughly.

3. Strain into Old-Fashioned glass over large square ice cube.

4. Garnish with star anise.

(Continued on page 56)

*To fat wash one 750-milliliter bottle of bourbon: pulverize 4 Chinese sausages in a food processor until the result resembles coarse bacon bits. Heat the sausage bits in a suitably sized skillet over medium-low heat, stirring consistently as they begin to sizzle slightly, taking care to not burn them (approximately 4 to 5 minutes). Add all sausage bits to bourbon and shake vigorously to combine. Move bourbon to refrigerator and let rest 4 to 6 hours until fat from sausage has solidified. Strain fat-washed bourbon through double-lined cheesecloth or coffee filter and store in refrigerator.

**To infuse 8 ounces of sweet syrup with five-spice powder, reheat sweet syrup in small pot over low heat with 1 cinnamon stick, 6 to 8 cloves, 3 star anise pods, ½ teaspoon Sichuan peppercorns, and ½ teaspoon fennel seeds for 5 to 6 minutes. Remove from heat and let infuse at room temperature for 1 hour, tasting every 15 minutes or so to ensure the flavor is to your liking. Strain out whole spices using *chinois* and store in food-safe container in refrigerator.

SCOTCH

Scotch offers a very distinctive earthy, smoky twang and is probably the most difficult to interchange between whisk(e)y cocktails due to its specific peat flavor (peat is partially decayed moss and vegetation that is prominent in the bogs and wetlands of Scotland). Scotch is categorized into five primary geographical regions, and the flavor profile of Scotch can vary widely based on the region from which the ingredients are sourced. While there are undoubtedly flavor variations from one distillery to the next within each region, generally speaking the flavor profiles of each region can be summarized as follows:

- Speyside: Smoky and complex with sweeter notes like apple and vanilla
- Highlands: Bold and full-bodied with flavors of peat, honey, and dried fruits
- Lowlands: Gentle and smooth with floral and sweet notes like toffee and cinnamon
- Islay: Known for its high-quality peat and characterized by strong smoky, earthy, and briny flavors (this also happens to be my personal favorite!)
- Campbelltown: Distinguished by its "wet wool" flavor along with smoke and brine

I chose these two recipes as they build nicely off that aroma to feel luxe and strong but are balanced enough to drink without the hot burn of alcohol. The recipes use blended Scotch, but don't let that stop you from substituting your favorite regional single malt if you'd like!

Golden Penicillin

When Jenny and I first started dating, she was a "clear liquors only" type of gal. Her standard order was a gin and tonic if she was feeling like a cocktail, which was an uncommon scenario in and of itself. Just as she pushed me out of my comfort zone with totally new foods—who knew jellyfish was so delicious?—I spent a lot of time finding new places and drinks to slowly open her up to a world of quality liquors and craft cocktails. One of the drinks she gravitated to early on was the Penicillin, a classic Scotch cocktail with blended Scotch with peat-forward Islay Scotch float, which completely took me by surprise given how smoky and (deceptively) boozy it is. Naturally, I learned to memorize this drink so I could conjure it up at home for us. This version replaces Islay Scotch with raw turmeric juice—an excellent digestif and anti-inflammation ingredient—that enhances the nutritional makeup and adds a gorgeous bright-orange hue.

INGREDIENTS

3 (⅛-inch-thick) slices ginger
½ ounce lemon juice
2 ounces blended Scotch
¾ ounce honey syrup
¼ ounce turmeric juice

INSTRUCTIONS

1. Muddle ginger in shaker with lemon juice.

2. Add Scotch, honey syrup, and ice.

3. Shake vigorously and double strain into Old-Fashioned glass with cocktail ice.

4. Use barspoon to carefully float turmeric juice on top.

Ode to Orkney

This cocktail was inspired by the classic Scotch drink called the Orkney Chapel. It's a fan favorite for its trinity of sweetness, smokiness, and nuttiness, but it is decidedly indulgent given its use of amontillado sherry, Grand Marnier, and dry vermouth (all of which are quite high in sugar). It's impossible to reproduce the original without these three pillars, so I didn't try to; instead, this cocktail pulls from the idea of building a stiff, dry, complex Scotch drink from sweet, sour, and bitter notes much like its namesake. I think you'll find yourself gravitating toward it after a big meal to wind down the night.

INGREDIENTS

2 ounces Scotch
½ ounce sweet syrup
¼ ounce apple cider
    vinegar
2–3 dashes orange bitters
Expressed orange peel,
    for garnish

INSTRUCTIONS

1. Add Scotch, sweet syrup, apple cider vinegar, and orange bitters to a mixing glass with ice.

2. Stir continuously until outside of glass is cold.

3. Strain into Old-Fashioned glass without ice.

4. Express orange peel over glass and add peel to glass.

RYE

The laws governing what makes an American rye whiskey are very similar to those for bourbon, with the exception of the main ingredient, of course. To be called American rye whiskey, the spirit must consist of at least 51 percent rye grain, be distilled at no higher than 160 proof, bottled at no lower than 80 proof, and aged in charred, new American oak barrels. Prior to Prohibition, rye was the king of whiskies in the United States. However, its relatively expensive ingredients and production process (and government subsidies on corn) limited the spirit's ability to rise back to prominence in the face of stiff competition from bourbon.

Rye has a sharper, stronger, and spicier bite than bourbon, but its richness and complexity allow it to mix more organically with the flavors of chocolate and honey. While some may be a bit put off by its more alcoholic (or "hot") taste, it's the perfect spirit for drinks that contain other sweet ingredients. I think it's great for spirit-forward cocktails that are meant to be enjoyed slowly. In fact, before the spread of bourbon's popularity and reach beyond the southern United States, many classic cocktails, such as the Manhattan, the Sazerac, and the Whiskey Sour, called strictly for rye.

Activated

In 2015, Jenny and I honeymooned across Southeast Asia for thirty days. We toured seven countries over the span of the month, staying too few days in each place but definitely eating two stomachs' worth of food each time. Let's just say at certain points of the journey, we *really* needed a little detox from our nonstop grubbing—which is when we learned of activated charcoal from a Thai American expat who happened to be seated next to us on the red wagons of Chiang Mai. (If you haven't been to Chiang Mai, Thailand, it has a great system of hop-on, hop-off red wagons that serve as public buses around the central parts of town.) In Thailand, activated charcoal is most often made from burnt coconut shells, readily available in pharmacies in the form of flattened cylinders that you chew and swallow. Back in the United States, you can also buy activated charcoal as a powder or in capsules. It's been long regarded as a cure for any gut-related ailment, as the charcoal binds to any toxins and forcibly expels them from your body. As a bit of a detox/retox, I've joined activated charcoal here with some nasal-clearing ginger, acidic lemon juice, and a shot of rye for an afternoon sipper that will ease you into a gut reset.

INGREDIENTS

3 (⅛-inch-thick) slices ginger
½ ounce lemon juice
1 ounce rye whiskey
½ ounce honey syrup
1 teaspoon activated charcoal powder

INSTRUCTIONS

1. Muddle ginger with lemon juice in shaker.

2. Add rye, honey syrup, and activated charcoal.

3. Shake vigorously and double strain into Old-Fashioned glass.

Hot Toddy

A Hot Toddy is a tried-and-true classic that's relatively low calorie and always comforting on a cold day. Lighting the cloves adds an extra hint of aromatic smoke and helps express the orange scent, but you can skip that step if fire is not your thing.

INGREDIENTS

1 orange peel
3 cloves
2 ounces rye
½ ounce sweet syrup
4 ounces boiling water

INSTRUCTIONS

1. Stud orange peel with cloves.

2. Combine rye and sweet syrup in cup or mug.

3. Add boiling water to mug and stir lightly to mix.

4. Light cloves on fire and let burn 2 seconds before dropping orange peel into drink.

IRISH WHISKEY

I was first introduced to Irish whiskey through the infamous Pickleback (a.k.a. the Bartender's Handshake). This drink, which consists of a shot of Irish whiskey chased down by a shot of pickle brine, is quite delicious (unless of course you don't like pickles) but also has the uncanny ability of completely masking the taste of the whiskey. It's like you didn't even have a shot at all! Or something like that. . . . If you've ever woken up the next morning after a night of picklebacks, it goes without saying that this is not the best way to be introduced to a liquor.

Fortunately for me, I was reintroduced to the spirit in quite possibly the exact opposite way—sipping high-end Irish whiskey at the No. 23 cocktail bar at the Merrion Hotel in Dublin as a nightcap after a long day's work (hey, that's what expense accounts are for, right?). Since that experience, I've had a fondness for Irish whiskey and have used it in many of my original cocktails. Irish whiskey has always had an interesting raisin-y flavor to me, and so I usually find myself using it in drinks where dried fruit and nuts are present. High-quality Irish whiskey is dry, smooth, and clean and can be paired well with many of the whisk(e)y recipes in this chapter.

Pistachio-Date Punch

I'm a sweets person. I could easily eat dessert for dinner, then some dessert for dessert—and occasionally, I actually do that. When Jenny and I went vacationing to Marrakech last year, we were en route to dinner at a Lebanese restaurant when we came across a sweetshop. It was filled with honeyed delights in intricate patterns like twisty flowers, etched domes, and springy bow ties. We somehow managed to exit the store with almost two pounds of treats, and they were so fantastic we munched on them as we waited for a table, snuck in some bites between courses, and then went back for a late-night fill-up after the fact. Two of my favorite pieces were a loopy flower made of date paste and a honey-and-pistachio roll, so I decided to turn this dessert experience into a dessert cocktail. While some may be put off by Irish whiskey, I found its directness to be a plus here, balancing the syrupy thickness of dates. This was my first time incorporating pistachio milk into a recipe, and I'm surprised it hasn't taken off—it's a beautiful pale green and is full of pistachio flavor, with a soft texture that feels more substantial, like oat milk. Even if you're not a sweets person, I think you'll be happy to drink this for an after-dinner treat.

INGREDIENTS

5 green cardamom pods
1 ounce date syrup*
1½ ounces Irish whiskey
2½ ounces pistachio
  milk**
⅓ dropper Ms. Betters
  Bitters Miraculous
  Foamer

INSTRUCTIONS

1. Muddle green cardamom pods with date syrup in BlenderBottle

2. Add remaining ingredients with ice.

3. Shake vigorously and strain with the *chinois* into an Old-Fashioned glass with a large square ice cube.

(Date Syrup and Pistachio Milk recipes on page 68)

*DATE SYRUP

(Yield 2 cups)

INGREDIENTS

1½ cup pitted dates
1½ cup water

INSTRUCTIONS

1. Add dates and water to blender and blend until smooth.

Note: The end result is a viscous syrup. For a more fluid result, use just 1 cup pitted dates to 1½ cup water.

**PISTACHIO MILK

(Yield 3 cups)

INGREDIENTS

1½ cup shelled pistachios
3 cups water
Pinch salt

INSTRUCTIONS

1. Soak the pistachios overnight in cold water in the refrigerator.

2. Add soaked pistachios, water, and salt to blender and blend until smooth.

3. Strain into an airtight container using a fine-mesh strainer or by pouring through a double-layered cheesecloth.

4. Discard the pulp or save for use in another dish

TEQUILA & MEZCAL

Tequila is a distilled spirit with a history dating back millennia. It is tightly regulated by the Mexican government; for a spirit to be classified as tequila, it must contain at least 51 percent Weber blue agave plant (the higher-quality brands use 100 percent) and can only be produced in certain municipalities of certain Mexican states, the most prominent of which is Jalisco, where the town of Tequila is located. The form of tequila we most often associate with the word is the clear, or "silver" or "*blanco*" tequila, that's either unaged or aged for less than two months. I find these to be beautifully clean, with herbaceous notes like green bell pepper and jalapeño and a hint of a sweet top note. Some consider the silver version of tequila the "healthiest" spirit option because it is lower in calories per shot than vodka or gin (~60 calories versus ~100) and supposedly has the fewest impurities of the clear liquors. While I personally don't advocate calorie counting, or substituting tequila for clear liquors anywhere you can, I do use this style of tequila often when creating health-conscious beverages that marry well with its taste and texture.

Tequila doesn't end at the *blanco* stage, however—aged varieties ("*reposado*" up to one year, "*añejo*" up to three years, "extra *añejo*" more than three years) are excellent choices in lieu of *blanco* as the various flavor compounds unravel and the alcoholic pang mellows over time. A final type of tequila is "*joven*" (young) or "*oro*" (gold) tequila, which most often comes unaged and flavored with caramel, oak, or other additives.

If you've ever had a bad night from tequila, then *joven* was likely the culprit. While there are certain high-quality brands of *joven*, they can be quite expensive and are best enjoyed unaltered either neat or on the rocks. Any of the recipes calling for silver tequila can easily be made with *reposado*, *añejo*, or extra *añejo* instead, depending on what final look and feel you're shooting for.

Mezcal (which can also be spelled as mescal) can be made from the heart (or "*piña*") of any varietal of agave—not just blue agave (a specification for tequila). The *piña* is then roasted before being fermented, usually over open flame in underground ovens, which gives mezcal its signature smoky tinge. The first distillation results in a "*joven*" mezcal that is clear, just like silver tequila, while wood barrel–aged versions—*reposado* or *añejado* for from two to nine months and *añejo* for at least one year—are softer, earthier, and darker. In recent years, mezcal has seen a surge of interest in the United States, and more brands all across the spectrum of age have become accessible across the market. I absolutely love mezcal—my standard order at a new bar is a mezcal Negroni—and love using it to impart a smoky edge to drinks that call for silver tequila. For those who may feel squeamish about the "worm" that lives in mezcal, don't worry: these mezcals (referred to as "*con gusano*" or "with worm") are not a given for every bottle of mezcal and also don't impact the final taste of the liquor. You can choose a bottle without one, or simply strain it out.

Sugar-Free Paloma

I have to admit: I typically don't enjoy the flavor of grapefruit at all—maybe I'm still shuddering from those awful grapefruit cups in school—but there's something about adding tequila that somehow renders it more tolerable. The bitterness of grapefruit is something many seek out to settle their stomachs, so I've created two recipes that I think make good use of both its citrus notes and its bitterness. The Paloma is a classic tequila drink that's already pretty healthy; I've removed the sugar completely so it can be a guilt-free brunch cocktail or after-dinner drink. The Hibiscus (page 79) is definitely moodier, especially if you use some mezcal, and plays well for heftier dishes or to cut through appetizers like olives and cheese.

INGREDIENTS

1½ ounces silver tequila

4 ounces fresh grapefruit juice

½ ounce lime juice

1 ounce grapefruit-flavored sparkling water

1 lime wedge, for garnish

INSTRUCTIONS

1. Combine tequila, grapefruit juice, and lime juice in shaker with ice.

2. Shake vigorously and strain into Collins glass with cocktail ice.

3. Top with sparkling water and garnish with lime.

Watermelon Mint Cooler

Watermelon is my absolute favorite fruit, and its season in North Carolina (where I went to college) marks the heyday of summertime festivities. There is truly nothing more refreshing than watermelon juice (especially when it's paired with mint) or a watermelon salad (with a touch of salt!) on a sweaty day lounging al fresco. These days I usually skip out on games of Greased Watermelon—in hindsight, a terrible waste of a good watermelon—and instead head to the bar to blend up fresh watermelon chunks for a nice beverage. Feel free to make this your own by adding some other fruit, or with a different base spirit, if you desire.

INGREDIENTS

5 sprigs mint
½ ounce lime juice
2 ounces fresh watermelon
    juice
1½ ounces silver tequila
1 sprig mint, for garnish

INSTRUCTIONS

1. Muddle mint and lime juice in shaker.

2. Add watermelon juice, tequila, and ice.

3. Shake vigorously and double strain into flute, coupe, or Nick and Nora glass.

4. Garnish with additional mint sprig.

Hibiscus

My second foray into the world of grapefruit is this drink, the Hibiscus. It's definitely moodier than the Paloma above, especially if you use some mezcal, and plays well for heftier dishes or to cut through appetizers like olives and cheese. If you're unfamiliar with hibiscus, it's a gorgeous flowering plant that's used in a variety of food cultures around the globe, often in the form of a beverage. The bright red-pink color is extracted using the petals of specific variety of hibiscus, and the flavor is very lightly tart.

INGREDIENTS

1½ hibiscus tea, chilled
1½ ounces silver tequila
  (or try half mezcal and
  half tequila for a slightly
  smoky treat!)
½ ounce sweet syrup
½ ounce grapefruit juice
1 grapefruit peel, for
  garnish

INSTRUCTIONS

1. Combine hibiscus tea, tequila, sweet syrup, and grapefruit juice in shaker with ice.

2. Shake vigorously and strain into Collins glass with cocktail ice.

3. Garnish with grapefruit peel.

Milk-Free Spiced Latte

At the ripe age of thirty-three, I discovered I had become lactose intolerant. I should've known this was coming, as all the men of my immediate family also became lactose intolerant in their thirties, but I suppose I had been hoping I would be an anomaly. For weeks, my stomach had been churning strangely after I ate certain foods—usually my evening indulgence of layered wafer cookies or Jenny's addictive candycap mushroom ice cream—so I finally did some A/B diet testing. Once I stopped eating any milk products, the grumbles and upset stomach disappeared. I was crushed. I didn't care too much for cheese, but what about cookies and milk? Pumpkin pie and ice cream? Or even an afternoon latte?

Even after I switched over to nondairy milks (pea milk has become my new favorite), I would look into other alternatives to achieve that creamy latte feel at home. Jenny alerted me to a recipe on ChefSteps, where they use xanthan gum to "whip" the coffee base, and I was intrigued. It's only a very small amount of xanthan, but the effect is significant *and* there is no impact on the final flavor. I've added some warming spices to this particular combination, reminiscent of some of the hot chocolates I've had in Mexico, but you can really use any spices you like or just keep it to plain coffee with a splash of liquor.

INGREDIENTS

6 ounces freshly brewed coffee
5 whole cloves
1 whole cinnamon stick
1 orange peel
½ ounce sweet syrup
1½ ounces *joven* mezcal
⅛ teaspoon xanthan gum
1 pinch ancho chile powder, for garnish
1 pinch ground nutmeg, for garnish

INSTRUCTIONS

1. Combine coffee with cloves, cinnamon, and orange in small pot over low-medium heat for 5 minutes.

2. Remove from heat, cover, and let steep for 15 minutes.

3. Strain coffee into blender and add sweet syrup and mezcal.

4. Start blender on low. Once vortex is moving, slowly add in xanthan gum, increasing the speed of the blender as you add more xanthan.

5. Once all xanthan has been added, turn the blender on high for 20 to 30 seconds to blend the mixture until foamy.

6. Pour into coffee mug of your choice and top with ancho chile powder and nutmeg.

Lessons from Nica

I didn't know there were multiple kinds of guava until I traveled to Nicaragua to put together a cocktail menu for a project for our nonprofit. I became enamored with the diversity of guava varieties: some were sour, others sweet, white to flushed red, textured and creamy. Sweet guavas were quite delicious to eat, but sour once, I found, were much more popular as beverages, and for good reason. Guava has a special perfume and weight that carries through the pucker and just grabs your attention. Admittedly, this recipe is difficult to make without the right guava, so it's not exactly a year-round drink, but I like to think of it as a special treat for when it finally is guava season.

INGREDIENTS

4–6 mint leaves
3 ounces White Indian guava and lime juice*
1½ ounces *añejo* tequila

INSTRUCTIONS

1. Muddle mint leaves with ½ ounce of guava lime juice in shaker.

2. Add remaining guava lime juice and tequila ingredients to shaker with ice.

3. Shake vigorously and double strain into an Old-Fashioned glass with a large square ice cube.

* Add flesh of one pink guava (make sure to remove the seeds!) and juice from two limes to a blender. Blend until smooth.

Recoverita

I don't think I could close off the tequila chapter without some sort of margarita, as it's become almost synonymous with the liquor itself. The OG margarita calls for orange liqueur, but since that's so high in sugar, I instead use a mix of tart cherry juice and pomegranate juice to recall the bitterness and acidity of orange—plus, tart cherry juice is great for muscle recovery, and pomegranate has lots of antioxidants. The cucumber may feel a little funny in combination, but I assure you that its brightness supplements that of the tequila and gives a great top note to the deeper fruit juices.

INGREDIENTS

2 cucumber slices
1 ounce lime juice
1½ ounces silver tequila
1 ounce pomegranate juice
½ ounce tart cherry juice
2 cucumber slices, for garnish

INSTRUCTIONS

1. Muddle cucumber slices with lime juice in cocktail shaker.

2. Add tequila, pomegranate juice, tart cherry juice, and ice.

3. Shake vigorously and double strain into Old-Fashioned glass with cocktail ice.

4. Garnish with cucumber slices.

Shots Trio

As I've gotten older, fun shots at the bar don't sit as well as they used to. But sometimes, life calls for some shots—and if we're being honest, they never really taste that great—so why not make them into tiny elixirs to preemptively stop potential hangovers? Ginger, turmeric, and switchel (vinegar) are all supremely great detoxes for your gut, but a little tough to manage on their own, so I mellow them out with bright ingredients like fennel or lemon and some natural sweetness like cantaloupe honey. And yes! There's still an ounce of alcohol per shot, so this is just as much of a "retox" as it is a detox.

GINGER MELON SHOOTER

INGREDIENTS

1 ounce bourbon
1 ounce fresh lemon juice
¼ ounce fresh cantaloupe
  juice
¼ ounce fresh ginger juice

INSTRUCTIONS

1. Combine all ingredients
   in shaker.

2. Stir to combine. Pour
   into a shot glass to
   serve.

FENNEL TURMERIC SHOOTER

INGREDIENTS

1 ounce vodka
½ ounce honey syrup
¼ ounce fresh fennel juice
¼ ounce fresh turmeric
  juice

INSTRUCTIONS

1. Combine all ingredients
   in shaker.

2. Stir to combine. Pour
   into a shot glass to
   serve.

TART CHERRY SWITCHEL SHOOTER

INGREDIENTS

1 once rye whiskey
½ ounce tart cherry juice*
½ ounce raw apple cider
  vinegar
1 pinch ground cinnamon,
  for garnish

INSTRUCTIONS

1. Combine all ingredients
   in shaker.

2. Stir to combine. Pour
   into a shot glass to
   serve.

3. Garnish with pinch of
   cinnamon.

*If tart cherry juice is not available, you can substitute cranberry juice.

RUM

Broadly speaking, rum is an overarching category of spirits created through the distillation of sugarcane juice or molasses (a sugarcane by-product). The most common form of the spirit carries the same name as the category "rum," and is produced using molasses. Rum is noticably sweeter than other liquors, given its foundation, and ranges from light (also called "silver" or "white," aged in stainless steel barrels for up to a year), to gold (also called "amber" rums, aged in wood barrels and typically combined with flavors or additives), to *añejo* (or aged rums, aged in wood barrels without additives), to dark rums (a subcategory of *añejo* rums distinguished by color, such as brown or red, that are aged in charred wood barrels.) As with tequila and mezcal, rums take on a more rounded body and marked enhancement of the caramel-y (especially molasses) flavors as it ages. Spiced rum, a category in itself, is quite popular in the States and usually has notes of warming spices and vanilla from the addition of spices like cinnamon and clove.

Since sugarcane originates from tropical climates, it's common for rum to usually be associated with (and the base spirit of) "tiki" style cocktails, an eclectic category of cocktails made with ingredients sourced within the same region—pineapples, coconut, oranges, and the like—served in carved cups that are loosely Polynesian-themed. I do love tiki cocktails, but I hate to pigeonhole rum into only that style of drink. It's a versatile liquor with a subtle sweetness that works well with sweeter, jammy fruits and in dessert-style cocktails. Premium rums can be a nice substitute in more spirit-forward cocktails like a Manhattan or Old-Fashioned, where the emphasis is really to let the nuance of the base liquor shine.

Another (narrowly defined and tightly controlled) type of rum is *rhum agricole*, sometimes called *rhum* for short. This rum must be produced in the French territories (most commonly, Martinique) and is distilled using fresh-pressed, locally grown sugarcane juice rather than molasses. *Rhum agricole* is decidedly more vegetal, earthy, and boozy (ABVs are commonly 50 percent or more) than its molasses-based cousin, so if you do want to add that hint of sugarcane to a more savory beverage, I recommend using *rhum agricole* or its Brazilian counterpart, cachaça, instead.

Coconut Water Colada

A beach vacation and piña coladas just go hand in hand. Jenny in particular has fond memories of ordering virgin piña coladas when on vacation with her family and sipping it from a giant pineapple with a cocktail umbrella. In this version, I've removed the extra fat of the usual coconut milk, instead using coconut water with fresh pineapple juice for its signature tropical flavor and the Miraculous Foamer to re-create the creaminess. You can serve this shaken and cold, or frozen if you want to blend all the ingredients together with ice, and serve in a coconut or pineapple.

INGREDIENTS

1½ ounce dark spiced rum
2 ounces coconut water
2 ounces fresh pineapple
    juice
½ ounce sweet syrup
½ ounce lime juice
⅓ dropper Mrs. Betters
    Bitters Miraculous
    Foamer

INSTRUCTIONS

1. Combine all ingredients in a BlenderBottle with ice.

2. Shake vigorously for 30 seconds.

3. Strain into a coupe or Nick and Nora glass.

Daiquiri

The Daiquiri is truly one of the most misunderstood classic cocktails in the world. The true version is deceptively simple, a drink served up containing only rum, lime juice, and demerara syrup. (Demerara sugar is a large-grained, light brown raw sugar with flavors of toffee and molasses. As an important aside, this is not the same as brown sugar, which is simply refined white sugar mixed with molasses.) The secret to a great Daiquiri is the balance of citrus, sweet, and liquor; the right ratio will make this cocktail novel, the wrong either a punch in the face or grossly sweet. My healthier expression of this cocktail is certainly different than the original, but I hope it still reinforces the notion that Daiquiris aren't slushy, alcoholic popsicles but a refined beverage worthy of making. The biggest change I've made is the rum type—because the sugar alternatives used in our sweet syrup are closer to white sugar in flavor, I've opted to use a dark rum to capture the richness and depth that demerara syrup would otherwise add.

INGREDIENTS

2 ounces dark rum
1 ounce fresh lime juice
¾ ounce sweet syrup

INSTRUCTIONS

1. Combine all ingredients in shaker with ice.

2. Shake vigorously and strain into coupe.

Frozen Strawberry "Daiquiri"

Now, there's nothing wrong with a slushy cocktail, either, if the occasion calls for it. When I think about my early experiences with American "daiquiris," I think of drinking yardsticks of the stuff at Señor Frog's on spring break. Sometimes, you may just want something fun and nostalgic to sip on as you relax on an inflatable floatie—but with this version, you can skip the raging hangover the day after. I've removed the artificial flavors and unnecessary sugars of the typical college-aged version and it's still as cold and easy-drinking as can be.

INGREDIENTS

2 ounces dark rum
¾ ounce sweet syrup
½ ounce lime juice
6–8 strawberries
1 cup ice

INSTRUCTIONS

1. Combine all ingredients in blender.

2. Blend until smooth and serve in a Collins or tiki glass.

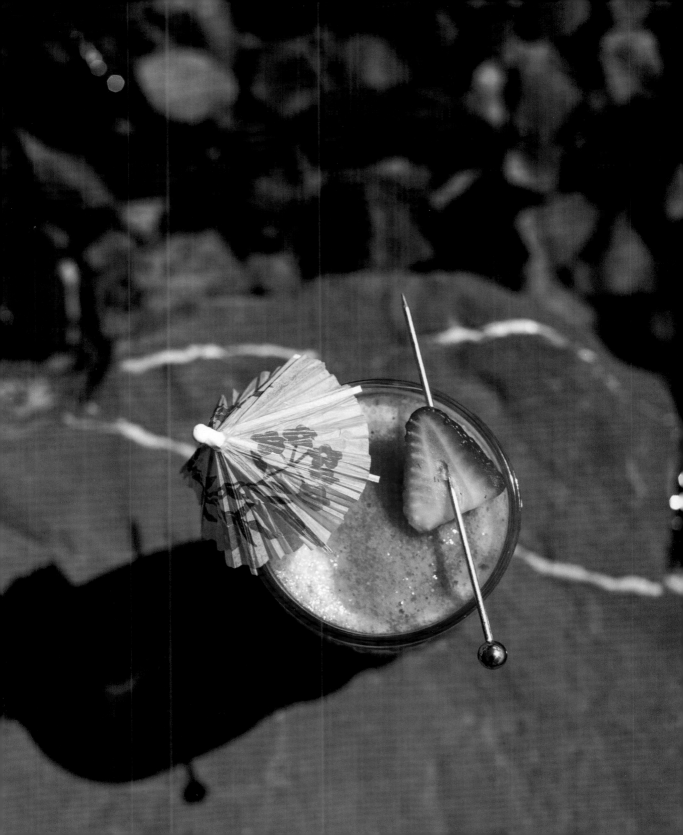

Dark 'N' Stormy

I know everyone's probably tired of me harping on classics, but they really are classics for a reason. The Dark 'N' Stormy was my introduction to rum in a cocktail, and it changed the way I looked at the alcohol entirely. This version removes the ginger ale and instead uses a combination of fresh ginger, sparkling water, and the bitterness of Angostura bitters to mimic the sweet, dry, tonic flavor. If you want to add something extra, garnish with some candied ginger.

INGREDIENTS

3 (1/8-inch-thick) slices
   ginger
1/2 ounce sweet syrup
2 ounces dark spiced rum
2 dashes Angostura bitters
3 ounces sparkling water
Lime wedge, for garnish

INSTRUCTIONS

1. Muddle ginger with sweet syrup in a shaker.

2. Add rum, bitters, and ice.

3. Shake vigorously and double strain into a Collins glass with ice.

4. Top with sparkling water and stir gently for 5 seconds.

5. Garnish with lime wedge.

Cuba Libre

Most people see Cuba Libre and think "Rum and Coke," but the two are far from being the same. Instead of just combining the alcohol and mixer together, a real Cuba Libre takes care to muddle fresh lime—peel on—to release the essential oils of the skin into the drink. Typically, the cola used is made from raw cane sugar, giving the drink richness and sweet-cooked notes a standard cola would not. Since we're opting for lower calories in this book, I choose a sugar-free cola and pair it with a dark spiced, or aged ("anejo"), rum to add complexity. But I encourage you to also try out the regular version with a quality rum and a Mexican Coke, because healthfulness is also about balance.

INGREDIENTS

1 lime
2 ounces dark spiced or
   anejo rum
4 ounces sugar-free cola

INSTRUCTIONS

1. Cut lime in half and squeeze the juice from both halves directly into Collins glass.

2. Put 1 half of lime into Collins glass and muddle lightly to release the oils from the rinds.

3. Add rum and ice to glass.

4. Top with cola and stir gently.

Avo "Toast"

What happens when you turn a millennial trend into a cocktail? This drink was actually made in jest, when Jenny suggested I make an alcoholic smoothie one morning when she was in a bad mood. We both laughed, and I promised her I would prepare her one for the next day using her regular smoothie ingredients. We were both surprised when this turned out pretty tasty, plus it contains a solid amount of dark leafy greens to (kind of) justify drinking so early in the day. The trick here is to really blend this until it is silky, otherwise the fibers of the kale against the backdrop of rum are decidedly not delicious.

INGREDIENTS

6 ounces coconut water
1½ ounces spiced rum
1 ounce lemon juice
1 ounce sweet syrup
2 cups kale, stemmed,
   chopped (30 grams)
½ avocado, pitted
   (35 grams)
1 medium banana
   (30 grams)
6 ice cubes

INSTRUCTIONS

1. Combine all ingredients in blender and blend until very smooth.

2. Serve in Collins glass with additional ice cubes and straw.

Spiced-Rum Milk Punch

Is a milk punch without milk still a milk punch? That's an existential question for the ages. As a newly lactose-intolerant mixologist myself, I admit I didn't realize how magical dairy was for cocktails until I couldn't drink it anymore. Its mouthfeel and flavor truly is hard to replace, but I've found there are certain cocktails that fare better with nondairy substitutes than others. This one I'm really happy with, as the milk plays second fiddle to the warming spices that boost this drink. In the winter months, this is also nice served hot and frothed.

INGREDIENTS

1½ ounces dark spiced rum
¾ ounce sweet syrup
3 ounces nondairy milk of your choice (I use unsweetened vanilla almond milk)
1 dash vanilla extract
⅓ dropper (approximately 3 milliliters) Mrs. Betters Bitters Miraculous Foamer
Ground cinnamon, for garnish
Ground nutmeg, for garnish

INSTRUCTIONS

1. Combine rum, sweet syrup, nondairy milk, vanilla extract, and Miraculous Foamer in BlenderBottle with ice.

2. Shake vigorously and strain with the *chinois* into coupe.

3. Garnish with pinch of cinnamon and nutmeg.

Mango Adventures

When Jenny and I were on our honeymoon, one of the places we traveled through was Bangkok. One of the main things Jenny was most excited to eat was mango sticky rice, but it was October when we arrived, and there was not a single mango in sight. After days of fruitless (pun intended) searching, we finally happened across one stall selling somewhat green-looking mangoes, at the ready with containers of cooked sticky rice with a to-go cup of coconut milk mixed with sweetened condensed milk. We both knew it was likely not to be the best mango we'd ever eaten, but after all that hard work, it still felt worthwhile to reward ourselves with a mango. So we bought one, went back to our hotel room, and pulled out little plastic chairs to sit on our patio and enjoy our half-ripe mango and sticky rice. We laughed as we speared the mango and our plastic forks bounced off the skin. It was such a great snippet from our adventures abroad, and this cocktail is meant to bring some of that spirit back to our everyday.

INGREDIENTS

1½ ounces dark spiced rum
3 ounces fresh mango juice
1 ounce coconut milk
½ ounce fresh lime juice

INSTRUCTIONS

1. Combine ingredients in shaker over ice.

2. Shake vigorously and strain into Old-Fashioned or Collins glass over ice.

OTHER BASE SPIRITS

Highlighting less commonly used spirits and ingredients is a critical foundation of my approach to mixology. While this section undoubtedly only scratches the surface, I couldn't write this book without at least giving a brief introduction to the world of possibilities opened up by lesser-known spirits. If you take one thing away from this book, I hope it's that mixology is an endless exploration in unmasking unique and unexpected flavors that suit your tastes and your lifestyle. These recipes are just the beginning—what will you find next?

The Green Hour

Absinthe is a liquor people are usually reluctant to use. Its history is mired in whispers of psychedelic properties (which was linked to a compound named thujone that is found in very trace quantities in absinthe but certainly not enough to cause any psychoactive reactions), and its distinctive flavor of licorice, anise, and fennel can easily outshine everything else it's paired with. I personally love the cleansing, earthy notes of absinthe and think it can be blended very well into a cocktail if it's given the right supporting actors. The "Green Hour" refers to the tradition passed on from France's belle epoque, when 5 p.m. denoted the time where people would flock to their local bars for a glass—or two, or three—of absinthe to start the evening.

Keep in mind absinthe is higher in ABV than other liquors—45 to 74 percent—so this cocktail is not for the faint of heart, but it does serve as a great introduction to the wonders this liquor can provide.

INGREDIENTS

5 mint leaves
½ ounce lime juice
1½ ounces absinthe
¾ ounce sweet syrup
1 mint sprig, for garnish
1 lime wedge, for garnish

INSTRUCTIONS

1. Muddle mint leaves with lime juice in shaker.

2. Add absinthe, sweet syrup, and ice.

3. Shake vigorously and double strain into Collins glass or Mule mug over ice.

4. Garnish with mint sprig and lime wedge.

Applejack Tea

Granny Smith apples have never been my favorite type of apple—I'm definitely a Gala or Fuji type of guy—but one day in early fall, the two of us went to a U-Pick farm in upstate New York for a day out of the city, and I found myself revisiting that sentiment. It was clear and cool as we wandered through the orchards, with varietals and varietals of apples—some of which I've never ever heard of—just bursting from the branches. For whatever reason, I felt compelled to tug off a Granny Smith from the tree and bite into it. It was dry and tart as always, but instead of turning my nose, I realized it could be a fantastic sour component for a cocktail. This cocktail was a fun experiment I didn't think would turn out to be so tasty—it's an excellent shakeup for when you're looking for a crisp white for a clambake or some raw oysters but want just a little more pucker.

INGREDIENTS

1½ ounces applejack or apple brandy

¾ ounce English breakfast tea syrup*

2 ounces fresh Granny Smith apple juice

½ ounce lemon juice

1 ounce dry champagne, prosecco, or similar sparkling white wine *or* sparkling water

INSTRUCTIONS

1. Combine applejack, tea syrup, apple juice, and lemon juice to shaker with ice.

2. Shake vigorously and strain into teacup.

3. Top with champagne.

*To make tea syrup, replace water in your desired sweet syrup recipe with English breakfast tea.

New Age Pimm's Cup

Seedlip is a brand of nonalcoholic spirits I've started using frequently as a base for zero ABV drinks. My brother and father are both now nondrinkers, so it's been exciting for me as a mixologist to be able to still create something custom for them to unwind with *and* serve it from my bar like a regular cocktail. While each of Seedlip's varietals have a certain flavor and can't be used interchangeably in the below recipes for New Age Pimm's Cup, Taste of the Tropics, and Mulled "Wine," I highly recommend you seek out other brands of nonalcoholic spirits—the category has been growing wildly!—to see if there are other pairings you enjoy in these recipes.

INGREDIENTS

2 cucumber slices, for garnish
1 orange slice, for garnish
1 lemon slice, for garnish
3 cucumber slices
1 orange wedge
1 lemon wedge
6 mint leaves
3 (⅛-inch-thick) slices ginger
½ ounce sweet syrup
2 ounces Seedlip Spice 94
½ ounce tart cherry juice
3 ounces sparkling water
1 mint sprig, for garnish

INSTRUCTIONS

1. Fill a Collins glass with ice and line the sides of the glass with cucumber slices, orange slice, and lemon slice, using the ice cubes to hold the garnishes in place.

2. Muddle cucumber slices, orange wedge, lemon wedge, mint leaves, and ginger in shaker with sweet syrup.

3. Add Seedlip, tart cherry juice, and ice and shake vigorously.

4. Double strain into Collins glass.

5. Top with sparkling water.

6. Garnish with mint sprig.

Taste of the Tropics

I first started experimenting with this combination of tropical fruit when I was creating some *baijiu* cocktails for an event Jenny and I were hosting. (*Baijiu* is a Chinese grain liquor typically distilled from fermented sorghum, rice, wheat, and other grains. It is actually the best-selling spirit in the world, with more liters sold per year than whiskey, vodka, and gin combined!) One of the defining characteristics of *baijiu* is its floral aroma, much like what you find in Seedlip's Garden 108, so as I kept tinkering with the cocktail I began to wonder if I could make the whole drink a mocktail. The combination was a hit with our "sober curious" friends, and it's also easy to batch up this cocktail to bring to whatever event you're invited to next!

INGREDIENTS

1 kiwi, peeled, chopped
1 ounce fresh pineapple juice
2 ounces Seedlip Garden 108
1 ounce fresh star fruit juice*

INSTRUCTIONS

1. Muddle kiwi with pineapple juice in shaker

2. Add remaining ingredients with ice.

3. Shake vigorously and double strain into Old-Fashioned glass with large square ice cube.

*If star fruit is not available, replace with more kiwi and add a squeeze of lemon.

Mulled "Wine"

Mulled wine is an absolute favorite during the holidays but is often cloyingly sweet to cover up shoddy alcohol. Between it and the spiked apple cider, those who may not want to drink often don't have any choice for a hot beverage. Since my father and my brother no longer drink, I figured this upcoming holiday would be a good time to debut a new, zero-proof mulled "wine" that brings forward much of the warmth of drinking—both physically and literally—but have none of the side effects. The addition of rosemary here is especially key, shifting the profile of this "wine" from only spiced notes to something more vibrant. If you're feeling a little wild, a sprig of lavender also works really well here.

INGREDIENTS

1 cup Seedlip Spice 94
¼ teaspoon whole allspice
¼ teaspoon pink peppercorns, crushed gently
¼ teaspoon whole cloves
2 lemon peels
6 orange peels
1 cinnamon stick
2 sprigs rosemary
Lemon or orange slices, for garnish
½ ounce sweet syrup (optional)

INSTRUCTIONS

1. Add all ingredients to small stockpot and bring to just under boil over medium-high heat.

2. Reduce to low heat, cover, and let simmer for 15 to 30 minutes.

3. Strain out the spices and serve warm in a glass mug or Old-Fashioned glass.

4. Garnish with lemon or orange wedge and other spices as desired.

5. Optional: Sweeten the mulled "wine" with ½ ounce sweet syrup.

Oceana

I mention aquavit (also spelled akvavit) briefly in the vodka chapter, but it's a liquor worth highlighting on its own. Aquavit is most popular in Scandinavia, and its signature infusion of caraway seed (or sometimes dill seed) makes it a great candidate for savory and herbal cocktails. This recipe originated from drinking Bloody Caesars (a Bloody Mary made with clam juice) but has since evolved into a totally tomato-free but still delightfully saline cocktail that integrates seamlessly into a charcuterie lineup or a spread of quality tinned seafood.

INGREDIENTS

1½ ounces aquavit
¾ ounce dill-infused sweet
   syrup
½ ounce clam juice
½ ounce lemon juice

INSTRUCTIONS

1. Combine ingredients in shaker with ice.

2. Shake vigorously and strain into Old-Fashioned glass with large ice cube.

ABOUT THE AUTHORS

Matt Dorsey is a modern-day renaissance man who operates as a finance executive by day and the head mixologist of Studio ATAO by night. After receiving his MBA from Columbia (where he met Jenny), Matt began a career in startups, joining Uber as an early member of its finance team before going on to serve as CFO of two startups. He has since struck out on his own as an independent consultant to early stage businesses. While building his career as a business professional, Matt also honed his skills as a self-trained mixologist, creating hundreds of original cocktails to pair alongside Jenny's food. He has won several cocktail competitions, including the 2015 Starchefs Cocktail Competition and the 2018 Edible Collective Cocktail Competition, and was a regional finalist for 2019's Woodford Reserve Manhattan Experience. He also implements interdisciplinary mediums in his work: a recent cocktail project within the Studio is named Ultimate First Date, an augmented reality-enabled cocktail that initiates a mobile "game" encouraging guests to have a radically intense conversation about everything from God to eugenics, utilizing the phone as a way to increase face time and engagement between people instead of detracting from it. His unique cocktail creations can be found on his Instagram @mixologistmattdorsey.

Jenny Dorsey is a professional chef, author, and artist specializing in interdisciplinary storytelling fusing food with social good. Her food is deeply symbolic, reaching beyond the realm of beautiful plating to actively explore topics like emotional vulnerability, the "othering" of immigrants, income inequality, cognitive dissonance, and familial estrangement. As the founder of nonprofit culinary production studio Studio ATAO, she often uses mediums such as virtual reality, poetry, spoken word, and interactive installation to deepen the guest experience both physically and virtually. Jenny's work and food has been featured on outlets such as Harper's Bazaar, NowTHIS, Eater, Food & Wine, Oxygen TV, and Food Network. She also writes and speaks professionally, often on the topics of food, identity and vulnerability. Her pieces have been published in outlets such as Narratively, Tasting Table, Michelin Guide and TechCrunch and she has spoken at conferences across the United States. Her full biography and portfolio can be found at https://jennydorsey.co

INDEX

CONVERSION CHARTS

Metric and Imperial Conversions
(These conversions are rounded for convenience)

Ingredient	Cups/Tablespoons/ Teaspoons	Ounces	Grams/Milliliters
Butter	1 cup/16 tablespoons/ 2 sticks	8 ounces	230 grams
Cheese, shredded	1 cup	4 ounces	110 grams
Cream cheese	1 tablespoon	0.5 ounce	14.5 grams
Cornstarch	1 tablespoon	0.3 ounce	8 grams
Flour, all-purpose	1 cup/1 tablespoon	4.5 ounces/0.3 ounce	125 grams/8 grams
Flour, whole wheat	1 cup	4 ounces	120 grams
Fruit, dried	1 cup	4 ounces	120 grams
Fruits or veggies, chopped	1 cup	5 to 7 ounces	145 to 200 grams
Fruits or veggies, pureed	1 cup	8.5 ounces	245 grams
Honey, maple syrup, or corn syrup	1 tablespoon	0.75 ounce	20 grams
Liquids: cream, milk, water, or juice	1 cup	8 fluid ounces	240 milliliters
Oats	1 cup	5.5 ounces	150 grams
Salt	1 teaspoon	0.2 ounce	6 grams
Spices: cinnamon, cloves, ginger, or nutmeg (ground)	1 teaspoon	0.2 ounce	5 milliliters
Sugar, brown, firmly packed	1 cup	7 ounces	200 grams
Sugar, white	1 cup/1 tablespoon	7 ounces/0.5 ounce	200 grams/12.5 grams
Vanilla extract	1 teaspoon	0.2 ounce	4 grams

Oven Temperatures

Fahrenheit	Celsius	Gas Mark
225°	110°	¼
250°	120°	½
275°	140°	1
300°	150°	2
325°	160°	3
350°	180°	4
375°	190°	5
400°	200°	6
425°	220°	7
450°	230°	8